A Life Lived and Laid Down for Friends

A Life Lived and Laid Down for Friends

A Progressive Christology

Don Erickson

RESOURCE *Publications* • Eugene, Oregon

A LIFE LIVED AND LAID DOWN FOR FRIENDS
A Progressive Christology

Copyright © 2019 Don Erickson. All rights reserved. Except for brief quotations in critical publications or reviews, no part of this book may be reproduced in any manner without prior written permission from the publisher. Write: Permissions, Wipf and Stock Publishers, 199 W. 8th Ave., Suite 3, Eugene, OR 97401.

Resource Publications
An Imprint of Wipf and Stock Publishers
199 W. 8th Ave., Suite 3
Eugene, OR 97401

www.wipfandstock.com

PAPERBACK ISBN: 978-1-5326-8246-9
HARDCOVER ISBN: 978-1-5326-8247-6
EBOOK ISBN: 978-1-5326-8248-3

Manufactured in the U.S.A.   SEPTEMBER 30, 2019

Grateful acknowledgement is made to Yale University Press for permission to reprint sections from *The New Testament: A Translation*, by David Bentley Hart, copyright © 2017 David Bentley Hart.

To Mom and Dad—
we didn't have much but you gave us all we needed,
most importantly your love and care.

Contents

Preface | xi
Introduction | xiii

Part 1 The Humility of the Nativity | 1

  1 Two Christmases | 3
  2 The Holy Family and Riches in the Rags | 8
  3 Apprentice to a Newborn | 13
  4 Bethlehem and Nazareth | 17
  5 Holding Cosmic Peace | 22
  6 Nativity's Interreligious Event | 26
  7 The First Carol | 29

Part 2 The Compassion of the Passion | 33

  8 Cleansing the Temple Sunday | 35
  9 Extremist in the Offense of Liberation | 40
  10 Passion and Transmitted Salvation | 45
  11 The Pluralist Paradigm of the Cross | 62
  12 Good Friday Blues, Easter Gospel | 71
  13 The Resurrection and Ascension's Wideness | 75
  14 Pentecost's Plan | 79
  15 My Confession | 85
  16 Christ's Bodhi Tree | 90

Part 3 The Wisdom of the Life | 97

17 Is Jesus the Only Way? | 99
18 Isn't the Kingdom of God Theocracy? | 110
19 Was Jesus Fine with Polytheists? | 115
20 Did Jesus Really Refer to Gentiles as "Dogs"? | 121
21 Did the Faith of a Group Get Applied to an Individual? | 127
22 What's the Difference between Humility and Humiliation? | 131
23 Did Jesus Give a Call to Arms? | 137
24 Was Jesus Anti-Family? | 140
25 Did Jesus Make a Heretic His People's Teacher | 144
26 Did Jesus Exclude the Samaritans? | 150
27 Who Is Excluded from the Commonwealth? | 158
28 Unforgivable-Sin Exclusion | 162
29 The Child Test | 164

Epilogue | 167
Bibliography | 171

Preface

This book developed out of sermons written and delivered while I was minister of the Community Church of North Orange and Tully (CCNOT), a small, rural church in Central Massachusetts. I was minister there for five years, between 2013 and 2018. It was my first pastorate and, to be frank, many of the sermons were much too academic for the setting. The church indulged me, for sure.

That said, I felt the ideas were worthy of being developed further and shared. This is what occurred in the past year since leaving the pastorate at CCNOT.

As the title and subtitle imply, this book is about Jesus the Christ. There have been thousands and thousands of books written about Jesus. Why the need for another? The answer to this question can best be elucidated by describing CCNOT. It is a federated New England church that joins together two church bodies, a United Church of Christ congregation and a Unitarian Universalist congregation. I saw one task of the pastor in this setting as presenting a Jesus that spoke to both religious traditions. The task was to present a Jesus that was both unique and earthbound, both revelatory and human. The book attempts to thread this needle as well.

I argue in this book that Jesus' contemporaneous uniqueness resided in his great love for his disciples, a love so profound that it led Jesus to sacrifice himself rather than see his disciples suffer. Jesus' death on the cross on behalf of the movement he led and on behalf of his followers was so transcendent that it influenced not only the birth of the church but the transcendence of the rabbi Jesus to divine status.

Simply put, I believe this book on Jesus offers a fresh look at a figure that still intrigues and is worshipped by millions. At least, my hope is that this book is not just another book about Jesus.

Preface

Before we begin, I would like to acknowledge some people who've been indelible to me as a person, a pastor, and now an author. I first want to thank spiritual teachers who've helped me to mature and develop a spiritual life as well as a love of ideas and learning. To Rev. Morgan Jones, my first mentor and pastor, for first instilling in me the love for God and for learning. To Rev. Steve Etner for not only baptizing me but also helping this working-class kid to see I was "college material." To Thich Giac Hai for teaching me that wisdom and compassion transcends religion and religious exclusiveness. To Dr. Kwangsoo Park for facilitating my writing and my study of the way of truth. And to Lance Smith for embodying the kind teacher and practitioner.

I also want to express my gratitude to professors that encouraged me to think, research, read, write, and be courageous throughout the creative process. To Dr. Gary Percesepe for teaching that following Jesus and struggling for justice and equality were by necessity mutually inclusive. To Dr. James Cone for speaking truth to power in a way unlike any other and encouraging me to not shy away from speaking hard truths. To Dr. Chung Hyun-Kyung for her matchless Buddhist-Christian voice and tenacious spirit. And to Dr. Richard Jaffe for urging me to work on the craft of writing and follow where the research and ideas lead.

I must also voice a thank you to the people of the Community Church of North Orange and Tully for indulging this rather nerdy pastor in my five years as your pastor. I especially thank Ward Johnson for his devotion and diligence and Pam Gale for her quiet wisdom and leadership.

Last but foremost, I want to thank my family: my parents, to whom this book is dedicated; my wife, Holly, whose love for and belief in me have often kept me going and thinking big; my son, Corey, who teaches me every day the power of resilience and joy.

Introduction

IN this work, I will use three terms a great deal more than others. I think it is only fair that I offer a few words about those words as I introduce the book. The words are self-emptying, compassion, and commonwealth. I believe the whole of Jesus Christ's teachings can be boiled down to those three words.

The first two words, self-emptying and compassion, I will use most often in tandem. Self-emptying basically means letting go of self or ego as one approaches the human life. To empty self while relating to others and the world is a sacred practice. Christ is described in Philippians 2 as the perfect example of self-emptying or kenosis in Greek. Paul describes Christ as a divine being who empties his divine self to become a lowly human servant. Christ's divine self-emptying gives way to his human humility and his self-sacrifice on the cross.

Humility is a term used in this book often as well. For the most part, humility is used interchangeably with self-emptying. Another related, synonymous term is selflessness. Jesus embodies all of these terms and calls on his followers to "be of the same mind" and heart.

Compassion is at the center of this book. Compassion presumes a practice of humility. In a way, adjoining self-emptying, humility, or selflessness with compassion is redundant. Compassion mandates humility, a letting go of one's own self to see and sense another's pain. Being with someone and experiencing their pain results from an initial "unselving." There can be no true compassion without first relinquishing sole focus on self and truly seeing and sitting with another in their pain. In feeling another's pain *with* them, the "with" makes all the difference. Going from "me fine alone" to "me hurting with" necessitates an other-self focus.

Introduction

Needless to say, though I will say it often, Jesus embodies compassion along with self-emptiness. And Jesus' embodiment of compassion changes everything.

Lastly, the term commonwealth is fundamental to this text. The "commonwealth of God" is a contemporary way to refer to the biblical term "kingdom of God." Because of the term commonwealth's novelty, I must spend some time in this introduction to discuss the term.

The reason I prefer the paraphrase/translation "commonwealth of God" is because it better elucidates what Jesus was getting at. Jesus' "kingdom" is not akin to kingdom as we know it, a run-of-the-mill kingdom ruled by human monarchy. The kingdom Jesus envisions indeed is a commonwealth.

Use of the word commonwealth comes from theologian John Cobb, who explains the rationale behind it:

> The Greek phrase that we translate as "kingdom of God" is *basileia theou*. A *basileia* is a politically defined region. It could be a kingdom, and indeed most of them were, but the term does not include that as part of its meaning. If you suppose in advance that God is like a king, then the *basileia* of God will certainly be a kingdom. But if God is like a father, then his region or land will not be a kingdom. We might describe a father's *basileia* better as the family estate. Depending on the kind of father we are talking about, that might be governed in various ways. When we consider how Jesus talked about God, the answer is that it would be managed for the sake of all who lived there with special concern for the weak and needy. We have no word for this, but my proposal is "commonwealth." Jesus' message is that the "divine commonwealth is at hand." Everyone should reverse directions and join in this new possibility. There is no reason to think of the God whose *basileia* this is, as a monarch![1]

Suffice to say, Jesus' commonwealth of God was the antithesis of the kingdom he was living in. The Roman Empire ruled the roost and did so with brute force and taxes levied. The poor were, of course, hit the hardest.

Religious communities were forced to pay their taxes and acquiesce in the face of the authority. The religious hierarchy learned to deal with this, and even thrived in the process. The common faithful found it harder.

The commonwealth Jesus preached amounted to heaven brought to earth. Jesus painted a portrait of this heavenly kingdom on earth,

---

1. Cobb, *Jesus' Abba*, 2.

Introduction

elucidating it as a completely new way of doing things and a new way of being in the world and in the face of empire. He sought "to comfort the afflicted and afflict the comfortable" and create a community built upon this paradigm. The primary tool for building this "beloved community," this commonwealth of God, is self-emptiness and compassion.

The arc of Jesus' life, as presented in the gospels, introduce these tools of building God's commonwealth in a poignant way. Jesus' birth, the Nativity story, presents the compassion of humility. Jesus' death, the Passion, offers up the humility of compassion. And Jesus' teaching ministry shows Jesus artfully using and fusing humility and compassion.

The three parts of the book follow this graceful arc. The first part will look at "The Humility of the Nativity." The second part will examine "The Compassion in the Passion." The third part will discuss Jesus' teaching ministry and his fusing of humility and compassion.

While the themes of self-emptying, compassion, and the commonwealth of God unite the chapters that follow, they don't necessarily build upon one another. It is my hope that continuity comes via the natural structure of the biblical text, which naturally serves as the foundation of this work.

I will be quoting from the gospels a great deal. I will mostly use a new translation of the New Testament by David Bentley Hart published by Yale University Press. Hart's translation will be my default translation. I will note when I am using a different translation.

Part 1

The Humility of the Nativity

— *1* —

Two Christmases

Christmas 2000, Iksan City, South Korea

On December 25, 2000, I took a walk down Daehagno, the college-town neighborhood across the street from the Korean university where I taught Conversational English. It was the first and only Christmas I've spent in a culture not Christian—or Christmas—centric. However, for me, that Christmas in Iksan, South Korea remains one of the most spiritually significant. It commenced a spiritual sojourn home.

Christmas not being a national holiday, all the shops were open in Daehagno. From one of the many shops "Silent Night" lilted, Frank Sinatra's 1957 rendition. That it was Ole Blue Eyes singing the beautiful carol only propounded my homesickness.

> Silent night, holy night,
> All is calm, all is bright . . .

The first four months of my year and a half in South Korea saw my Buddhist practice growing deep roots. I immersed myself in the Buddhism of Korea. I visited Buddhist temples every chance I got. I informally studied with a professor of Buddhism at the university campus where I taught, Wonkwang University. I meditated as often as I could.

Despite this, or maybe *because* of this, my connection to the figure of Jesus reawakened within me. Buddhist practice is powerful that way. It moves you to look deep at where you come from, at where the hurt and the discord is, and helps forge a path to contentment.

Moreover, when you are in unfamiliar territory and cultural differences and culture shock pervade, it is only natural you seek what is safest and most familiar and feel comforted when it's found. Jesus, just the name, still felt safe, familiar, and comfort giving.

> Shepherds quake at the sight
> Glories stream from heaven afar
> Heavenly hosts sing "Alleluia"!

The streets of Daehagno did not exactly stand silent that Christmas night. Virtually all the shops were open and busy. No snow fell. No brighter than usual streetlights christened. No enlightenment ignited by stars shooting across the sky. Only the feeling that I was remembering something I once knew by heart and in my heart but had forgotten.

Ever since I parted ways with Christianity in the mid-90s, Christmas increasingly seemed unimportant. It loomed as a capitalist enterprise enjoyable to the children who did not know the difference. And like an artificial Christmas tree, I placed Christmas in the cluttered basement of my mind along with my disillusionment, and I had no plans of ever bringing it out again. Christmas was simply not pertinent. I refused to let it be, for it had let me down and kicked me out. I did not trust the Christian faith and did not see ever trusting or entrusting it.

What's more, my departure from Christianity had complicated my relationship with my family. I was no longer the evangelical Billy Graham-to-be or the great young Christian hope of my church. In fact, I was implicitly excluded though my doubt was sincere and answer seeking. My isolation both angered and hurt.

Thankfully, the silence of that moment in a South Korean college town, the music of a Sinatra serenade wafting from a store, released something within me.

> Radiant beams from Thy holy face
> with the dawn of redeeming grace.
> Jesus, Lord, at Thy birth . . .

As the sound of "Silent Night" faded, I silently cried as one sense of isolation, that of straying from the faith of my family, gave way to another. An isolation less created, more inevitable.

Despite my best efforts, I could not understand most of the language spoken by the Korean citizens of Iksan passing me by. I could not find full inclusion in the culture I now lived within. Even the Buddhism I encountered seemed sometimes like a second language, one I had difficulty understanding.

Yet I understood what Sinatra was singing.

This understanding in turn moved a longing for home in every sense of the word. I wanted home to insulate me. I wanted the safety found there, away from my isolation.

> Son of God, love's pure light,
> Radiant streams from thy holy face,
> with the dawn of redeeming grace . . .

Amid my spiritual homesickness, Christmas truths began to reveal themselves. Jesus arrived narrativeless, storyless, languageless, ambitionless. Jesus was revealed to and through a young, anonymous family struggling to find their way. Jesus entered a society impoverished and oppressed, one enduring the acute reality of suffering.

At the same time, infant Jesus, by his very nature, arrives enlightened and salvation bearing, turning all expectations on their heads. Jesus' liberation-bearing birth subverts what was envisaged in a spiritual hero, whether it be a prophet, messiah, buddha, or bodhisattva.

With this holy infant there is no plotted climb to spiritual prowess or political power. There is no need for spiritual ambition, a striving to attain prominence or prestige as a religious teacher or leader. As a mere infant, baby Jesus teaches and shows us all we need to know and subverts the world's notions of spiritual ambition and religious hierarchy.

A child shall lead us. And that child is here in our midst. Learn the way of the child.

This was the good news I was beginning to internalize as I walked the streets of a Korean city in the beginnings of winter. The truth of divine humility and newness with us, this was the Christmas story reborn within me as Sinatra crooned of Christ.

Finding room for Jesus in the inn of my heart would thereafter be my living koan, my way to salvation. It was a way of salvation initially pondered in Korea, the beautiful land of morning calm, its many mountains standing as wind-filled monuments to the search.

Christmas 2001, New York City, U.S.

In addition to the Christmas carols, chaos, and commercialism, and in spite of 9/11's fresh wounds, James Cone's voice, a uniquely piercing and powerful voice, was ringing in my ears. I had just completed his Systematic Theology 101 class that first semester at Union Theological Seminary, a rite of passage for any Union student. And like many rites of passage, it was not always easy or painless for this privileged, White, Protestant male.

Dr. Cone saw it as his rightful duty to give notice to especially the White seminarians in his class that sitting idle and playing preacher was not enough. He drilled into us that God is not White. And Jesus was not White, and in fact was "ontologically Black." Christ was Black in that enslavement, oppression, and lynching are central to the divine story and baked in the cake of the Christian gospel. And this was true from the very beginning—of Genesis and of Jesus of Nazareth and his birth. To be a White preacher preaching Christ meant being in solidarity with all that Christ was. And Christ was ontologically Black.

As I walked up Broadway after lunch at Mil Korean Restaurant, I internally heard the voice of Dr. Cone: "You're going to go home and have your Christmas parties and dinners and presents. Somewhere in there, you're going to celebrate the birth of baby Jesus and maybe even go to church. Now, you might not hear this in your church, but I want you to remember. That baby Jesus, that baby was a Black Middle-Eastern baby born to Black Middle-Eastern parents in a poor town along the Galilee. That Black baby was born in a time of empire, on the other side of it, too. Jesus wasn't born in Rome, now. Jesus was born in Judea, which Rome occupied and oppressed and abused. In other words, Jesus wasn't born in America. No, no. Jesus was born in Afghanistan or Palestine or Central America. I think you see where I am going . . . There wasn't nothing White about that first Christmas."

These words were ringing in my ears. A bell, a black, proud, dissonant Christmas bell blaring out truth.

Yes, Jesus was the Everychild. But he was also and unequivocally a child of color. To ignore the latter, the particular, in favor of the former, the universal, was to do the Christmas and the Christian story injustice. It would do to the story what the forces of oppression do to the poor and the most vulnerable—make them invisible.

Two Christmases

And it was Jesus, a dark-skinned Palestinian Jew, who experienced the life of the persecuted, the maligned, the rejected, the ridiculed, and eventually the lynched. It was this Jesus in his own particular time and place that came to liberate a people—his people—and in turn the world.

— 2 —

The Holy Family and Riches in the Rags

The story of the Nativity, like the whole story of the Jesus movement, is a story of misfits. It is a story of misfits who, despite paralleling their religious tradition, never find full belonging in their community. It is a story of misfits who lay a new foundation, one that eventually changes the world.

In the beginning, there was Mary. As the story goes, she is a young, engaged "maiden."[1] According to the story, an angel named Gabriel appeared to her and told her of the news that she will bear a messiah.

Mary is said to be betrothed to Joseph. She is promised to Joseph, and this betrothal is legally binding.

Marriage followed betrothal and amounted to the moment when the woman moved in with the man and marital relations commenced. This usually came a year after the binding engagement known as betrothal. Marriage was expected to happen before a woman was eighteen years of age but often happened much earlier for poorer families, as was the case with Mary.

There were to be no marital relations in that year between the betrothal period and marriage. If such relations did happen, and it was found out, there could be severe, even lethal consequences. A strict reading of the religious texts meant stoning.

---

1. Matthew 1:23, which begins, "behold, the virgin shall conceive," borrows from Isaiah 7:14. However, the Hebrew word used in Isaiah is *almah*, which means "maiden"—"behold, a maiden shall conceive"—and does not by necessity imply virginity.

Premarital Conception

Whatever the case may be, Jesus was conceived while Joseph and Mary were betrothed and before they were married. Before Jesus is born it is presumed Mary and Joseph get married quickly and quietly.

So, Mary is a young bride, much younger than eighteen. And she quickly begins to show. People in the neighborhood put two and one together, as they always do, and the presumptions began. People presumed Jesus was conceived out of wedlock. He was. And few people believed the Spirit had anything to do with it.

As we can imagine, all of this brought disgrace. Joseph felt the disgrace, certainly. But Mary, full of grace, felt *dis*grace. The patriarchal quip of "boys will be boys" must have been heavy in the air along with the judgmental declaratives that "girls must be strong."

From this point on, Joseph and especially Mary would have been looked down upon in the neighborhood, seen as morally impure, weak, sinful. They were likely shunned, dismissed, mistrusted. They were likely the subject of gossip going around town, things said behind their backs with eyes askance.[2]

Mary withstood the community's judgment. Full of faith, she persisted, stubbornly believing she was worthy, that she was chosen by God, that she was called upon to bear the Anointed One. This speaks to Mary's great strength and her sacred subversiveness. We see this clearly in Mary's words upon hearing the news of the new messiah she would bear. It comes from Luke 1:45–55:

> My soul proclaims the Lord's greatness, And my spirit rejoices in God my savior, Because he looked upon the low estate of his slave. For see: Henceforth all generations will bless me; Because the Mighty One has done great things to me. And holy is his name, And his mercy is for generations and generations to those who fear him. He has worked power with his arm, he has scattered those who are arrogant in the thoughts of their hearts; He has pulled dynasts down from thrones and exalted the humble, He has filled the hungry with good things and sent the rich away empty. He has given aid to Israel his servant, remembering his mercy, Just as he promised to our fathers, to Abraham and to his seed, throughout the age.

---

2. Chilton, *Rabbi Jesus*, 5ff.

Riches in the Rags

We should also remember the same negative feelings toward Mary and Joseph would have been passed on to the child. Jesus would have been seen by some as illegitimate. He would have been seen as somehow sullied by the nature of his conception. He would have been denigrated and shunned and discriminated against too.

When you consider how the community would have responded to the situation, you realize how remarkable the Christmas story is. It is not a rags-to-riches story. It is a riches-are-in-the-rags story.

Riches are embedded in the so-called rags of society. God is most profoundly seen and realized in people like Mary and Joseph and Jesus. That is the scandal of the Christmas story.

Despite all the odds and the ridicule toward them, it is the last that are first, it is the lowly that are exalted, it is the poor that are blessed. It is a story of resistance against not just the powerful, as we see in King Herod being figuratively dethroned by Jesus. It is a Jewish story of resistance against the condemnatory judgment, self-righteousness, and moralistic animus that too often defined the society Jesus was born into.

The Nativity story is a defiant marker that says, yes, the powerful think they will remain that way and the judgmental may think they are better than everyone else, but God favors the lowly, the humble, the poor, the outcast, the shunned. In them, through them, God chooses to speak the Word.

A Jewish Nativity

This Nativity story is a deeply Jewish story. It follows a theme that we find throughout the Hebrew scriptures. The theme amounts to God taking the outcast, the down-and-out, the hopeless, and using them as vessels to fulfill God's promise. This theme that there is richness in the rags pervades the Hebrew scriptures.

- Adam and Eve—they fall, but are not forgotten and from them comes Abraham.
- Abraham and Sarah—old, barren, and hopeless, as scripture tells us, but in whom God finds favor and from whom a nation is born

- Jacob—deceives his father into getting the family's inheritance, pridefully fights with the angel of the Lord, yet God chooses him to be the patriarch of his people.
- Moses—an adopted Egyptian who in a fit of rage kills an Egyptian boss who is abusing his Hebrew employee. Moses becomes a fugitive and is eventually found in the field, working as a shepherd. God chooses him to free his people from slavery.
- David—a shepherd too, a loner, a philanderer (remember Bathsheba?), and complicit in an assassination, but God chooses him as king and he becomes the greatest king Israel ever had, the one Jews still look to as the benchmark.
- The Prophets—rebellious outcasts and troublemakers whom God uses to speak truth to his people.
- The Hebrew people—despite their moments of bickering, ingratitude, and even idolatry, God remains faithful and gracious to them, seeing them as his own no matter what.

The same theme continues in the New Testament beginning with Mary, an unmarried teenage mother; Joseph, the so-called "wronged husband" who is paying the penalty of isolation; and Jesus, the perceived illegitimate son of this poor family from Nazareth, itself seen as the backwater of Judea. From this family in the "nowhere of Nazareth" comes a new message, a new picture of grace that will literally turn the world upside down.

The theme is continued in Peter, the thrice-denier of Jesus and the one who flees his teacher in his darkest moment. Peter becomes the rock upon which the Christian church is built. Thomas, the doubter always needing proof even when it makes him look foolish, faithfully brings Christianity to Asia. Paul, a persecutor of Christians and accomplice to the killing of Stephen, becomes the greatest missionary in the history of Christianity.

The Working-Class Founder

My last point on the Nativity story is this: when you consider the birth stories of other founders of religions (Judaism doesn't technically have a founder), you see how remarkable the story of Jesus' birth is.

A parallel to Christ's birth story is the Buddha's birth story. Like Jesus, the Buddha was born supernaturally, not to a virgin but to a thirty-year-old wife who was at the time celibate. In other words, both Jesus and Buddha are described as born void of the act that normally brings about a baby.

The similarities end there. The Buddha's mother, Maya, was married and she conceived the boy twenty years into her marriage. Marital relations would have been presumed. There would have been no feelings of shame involved. Maya was not shunned like Mary was.

Another big difference is that Maya and her husband were the equivalent of aristocrats. The Buddha's father, Suddhuano, was an important, honored leader of his province and clan. The Buddha was born into a rich and powerful family.

With the Buddha we have a son born into a powerful, respectable, aristocratic family. With Christ we have just the opposite. Jesus is born to a powerless, poor, and morally suspect—in the community's eyes—family. Buddha was seen as a kind of prince. Jesus was seen as an illegitimate child.

Maybe it's the iconoclast in me. Maybe its my tendency to root for the punk-rocking underdog. Maybe it's the bleeding heart in me. I don't know. But Jesus' story simply resonates more. I easily see myself in the perceived losers, in the wrongly maligned, in the misunderstood Mary and Jesus. I identify with the God-loved and God-favored misfits who change it all, who threaten and eventually topple an empire, who continually tell us that it is the losers who point to the way of truth and compassion.

Many would say that the Christian story is a very American story. However, what is different with the Christian story is that Jesus never rises to wealth or power. In fact, Jesus critiques the very idea that there is a rise involved in wealth or power. We *rise* when we give wealth away and share power with others. The Christian life means rising to humility in all aspects of life.

Again, Jesus Christ's story is not a rags-to-riches story. It is a story that preaches the good news that richness is found in the rags here and now. This Christmas truth transforms the world in every step and breath along the way.

— 3 —

Apprentice to a Newborn

Jesus and the shepherds are central to our Christmas crèches. Jesus and the shepherds go together. They go together in the climax of the Nativity story. Jesus and the shepherds are tied together and will be so forever.

Why? Why shepherds, the lowliest occupation there was in Jesus' time? Why does God give the good news about Jesus' arrival to the shepherds before anyone else outside family? Why are the shepherds the first neutral party to hear the gospel?

There are a few reasons, I'd say. I give them quickly before I get to the heart of what I want to discuss.

The Shepherds Rationale

The shepherd was indeed the lowliest of occupations. To be a shepherd in Jesus' day was the equivalent of being a fast-food employee. The gospel comes first to that society's Burger King, Dairy Queen, and Little Caesars employees. Liberation to the poor and exaltation of the least in society begins from the very beginning, right there at the manger.

In addition, John the Baptist, Jesus' cousin, will later call Jesus "the lamb of God who takes away the sin of the world." So, the shepherds come to see this new lamb who will change their lives. Shepherds do the work of midwifing lambs. Hence, shepherds are chosen.

Moreover, there is the even-then-revered scripture we know as the Twenty-Third Psalm—"The Lord is my shepherd, I shall not want." The Gospels will also later point to Jesus as the Good Shepherd. So, the shepherds are also coming to visit a fellow shepherd, the shepherd's shepherd, the shepherd of all shepherds, the Good Shepherd. The shepherds are coming to learn from the master.

But an even more telling reason for why it is shepherds that God first reveals the good news to is seen in Jesus' lineage. Jesus is the son of David and the new David who will take the throne as king of Israel and "make Israel great again."

And who was David? A shepherd. The shepherds represent David. David in the form of the shepherds comes to confirm that here is the New David, the awaited Anointed One, the child king of Israel. David via the shepherds is blessing and anointing Jesus, passing the torch to this babe king.

We, the Shepherds

When it comes to our own spirituality, when it comes to our relationship with God, what is the importance of all of this shepherd talk? Who cares that it was to shepherds that God came first?

Well, we are called to follow Christ, the Good Shepherd. We are called to be disciples of Christ. That word "disciple" we might also term "apprentice." We are called to be apprentices of Christ. Relatedly, we are called to imitate Christ, to follow in his way, apply what we learn as his apprentices, and become good shepherds ourselves.

Christ's later relationship with his disciple Peter makes this clear. Peter in many ways is a stand-in for all of us. Peter in the Gospels is an everyman, an imperfect, sometimes loud and obnoxious bloke who falls, fails, and denies. Yet in the process of following Jesus, Peter is changed.

After the resurrection, Peter, amid his grief of denying his teacher, reconciles with Jesus. This reconciliation comes via Jesus' command that Peter "shepherd his flock." Interesting, the word translated "shepherd" is the Latin word *pastor*. Jesus commands Peter to "pastor his flock."

As disciples called to make disciples of all nations, we are called to pastorship as well. We are called to bring others into the fold of the commonwealth. We are called to be pastors like Christ, the Good Pastor.

This is to say we are meant to be the shepherds in the Nativity scene. We are called to be the shepherds in the story looking for joy and peace to be born unto us and in us. We are to be the lowly shepherds seeking meaning and hope.

And this one in the manger, this newborn, is the Master. This newborn is the Master Shepherd we are called to be the apprentice of.

The prophet Isaiah talked about a child that shall lead us. "The wolf will live with the lamb, the leopard will lie down with the goat, the calf and the lion and the yearling together; and a little child will lead them."

Jesus is this little child, the Christian tradition tells us. This little child leads us and teaches us, all from a lowly manger, an ad hoc home void of four walls, a ceiling, or even a crib.

We look to this little child. We—the shepherds—are the apprentices. What are we meant to learn? What does this infant Jesus teach us? What does this infant Jesus show us about leadership? Are we present enough to see? What do we see when we are still enough?

Followers of the Child

If we are still, we realize Jesus' mere presence teaches, guides, leads us. This infant is Immanuel, God newly with us. And our internalization of this newness with us is the first step. A first step means we are walking.

If we are still, we observe that this infant lives without thoughts about the past or the future. This infant resides in the moment. This infant does not judge nor ponder things for too long but simply breathes in and out with us, letting us know what we need to do by simply being. This baby Jesus teaches us the gift of merely being present.

If we are still, the little one cooing there in the manger teaches us that there is power in vulnerability, there is power in letting love feed and nurture us. Such vulnerability exemplifies and leads to the divine realm of God.

My Apprentice Is a Jewish Child

Our mentor, the infant shepherd we seek to apprentice us, *is* us, is like us, is just as vulnerable, just as weak and needy, just as prone to falling and losing.

The holy family of baby Jesus, Joseph, and Mary would not be called winners of life then or now. Those in high places then and now don't find much alluring in this Jesus, this Jesus who, to help others find victory, becomes the loser. The paradigm of becoming the loser for the sake of others' salvation is seen from the very beginning.

Jesus is not a fortunate one. He is a child not fortunate enough to be born in a room, not even a room in a shoddy motel, and surely not a Trump hotel. Jesus is born in the barn outside of them.

Jesus is a child born amid farm animals and sleeping in a feeding trough. His parents soon will flee as refugees to Egypt to escape the persecution and violence of their government. Far from victors in the world's games of reality TV, Jesus and his family are victims, victimized by raw power, hate, and violence.

And so, from the crib to the cross, Jesus will walk the way of the lowly Good Shepherd. He will defy raw power by being a servant. He will overcome hate with love. He will resist violence with nonviolence. He will accept victimhood and win our victory. As the ultimate victim, he becomes the ultimate victor. And through him salvation is given, and sin and death defeated completely, in total, with "It is finished."

We are called to be this Good Shepherd's apprentices. We are called to sit at the foot of the Master cooing awake in a manger and learn the way of simple love.

Look past the Christmas clutter and the crass chaos around us. Look to the one we celebrate, the one lying in a manger as vulnerable and frail as a newborn can be. See a lesson in the fragile moments of that newborn's presence. This tender moment, this tender one here to save us, namely from ourselves, this vulnerable one here trumps all pride and greed and ignorance. This innocent one extinguishes the fires of hell with the light of hope. This humble one present with us, he apprentices us with priceless grace, renewed life, and endless love that helps us to in turn love God and others. Receive the gift and live accordingly.

— 4 —

Bethlehem and Nazareth

Rust-Belt Town Prototypes

I GREW up in a small city a hundred miles north of New York City called Hudson, New York. Not Croton-on-the-Hudson or Hastings-on-the-Hudson, but Hudson on the Hudson. In high school, my family moved to an even smaller town, a boondock town at the foothills of the Catskill Mountains called Earlton. Like most towns in the vast Upstate New York region, both Hudson and Earlton perpetually struggled, perpetually bearing economic recession. Hudson had a reputation as a rough-around-the-edges kind of town. And Earlton was farmland long forgotten.

The first church I pastored resided in a tiny village between two New England towns. A year or so into that pastor position, one of those local top-ten lists was going around on Facebook. It was titled "The 10 Most Redneck Towns" in the state. The reason I noticed it was that the #1 redneck town, according to so-called "scientific scoring," was one of those towns just down the road. Another list from a couple years before included the other neighboring town as one of the worst places to live in the state.

This negative reputation was widespread. During my ministry in that tiny village, I regularly met with a group of ministers who served churches in the suburbs and exurbs of Boston. When I first mentioned where I lived and ministered, one minister's response struck me. The minister's eyebrows went up and a disconcerted look came upon his face. Then he said: "Hmm, interesting town. At least you have [a swankier college-town] close by."

Bethlehem, Rust-Belt Town Prototype I

If someone were doing a ranking of ancient Palestinian towns in Jesus' day, Jesus' hometown of Nazareth would certainly be on some kind of "worst places to live" or "redneck towns" list. So would Bethlehem, the small town in which Jesus was born. They were ancient Palestinian examples of those down-on-their-luck New England towns or Hudson or Earlton.

Bethlehem was a town long past its glory days. Yes, it had some religious importance. King David, the greatest king the Jewish nation ever had, was from Bethlehem. It was known as the City of David. Bethlehem was also once known as the town that took in Jews escaping captivity in ancient Babylon.

However, by the time Jesus was born, it was a town on the outs. Joseph, the human father of Jesus, left Bethlehem for this reason. There were no jobs, no opportunity, no long-term security in Bethlehem. The only reason Jesus was born in Bethlehem was because there was a census that mandated men of the household return to their hometowns for their households to be counted.

Nazareth, Rust-Belt Town Prototype II

Jesus did not grow up in Bethlehem, however. He grew up in Nazareth, an even humbler, harder-scrabbled town.

Of all places to have a heroic messiah to come from, Nazareth would be very low on the list. Biblical historian Bart Ehrman says this about Nazareth: "It was far too small, poor, and insignificant. Most people had never heard of it and those who had heard didn't care. Even though it existed, this is not the place someone would make up as the hometown of the messiah."[1]

The Bible itself points to this reality. In the Gospel of John, one of Jesus' soon-to-be disciples, Nathaniel, is incredulous that the messiah could come from Nazareth. Nathaniel, after hearing of Jesus' hometown, quips, "Nazareth! Can anything good come from there?"

We might say Nazareth had the stereotype Hudson, New York had. Nazareth was a working-class town always struggling to get by.

Like small New England towns in relation to Boston, or Hudson in relation to New York City, citizens of Nazareth knew about Jerusalem. They

---

1. Bart Ehrman. "Did Nazareth Exist." par. 13

monitored the news coming from Jerusalem, visited Jerusalem, yet at the same time Jerusalem was a world away.

The issues and society of urban Jerusalem did not register in a deep way in the lives of rural Nazarenes. Like any rural town near tremendous metropolises like Jerusalem or Boston or New York City, rural towns had a love-hate relationship with "the city." Bubbling beneath it all was an animosity that said, you in the city get all the limelight, get all the power, get all the money. And here we are, living lives you all know nothing about, don't want to know anything about, and ignore in every way. Do you even know we exist? Does Massachusetts stop at I-495? Does New York stop at Yonkers or Rockland County?

Jesus, the Craftsman

Jesus sensed, heard, and experienced this sentiment all around him. He probably felt it himself. This is especially true because of the family he grew up in. His father was blue-collar before there were collars.

Joseph and Jesus used their hands. Those hands were rough and calloused and weather and work-worn. Their skin was dark and leathery from the close Middle East sun. They came home for dinner soaked in sweat and wearied by work.

We traditionally have viewed Joseph as a carpenter, a craft that Jesus followed in. However, there is a better translation for the Greek word usually translated as "carpenter." "Craftsmen" is a better translation. Joseph and his apprentice-son Jesus were craftsmen or general contractors.

When Joseph and his family did travel to Jerusalem or to wealthier neighboring towns, they got the real story, how people in Jerusalem thought of "their kind." Joseph and family understood this sentiment. They were from Nazareth. Nazareth compared to Jerusalem or to Galilee was like night and day. Nazareth was poorer, less educated, less hopeful. And Nazareth had a reputation as the ancient Palestinian equivalent of "redneck country."

And, as has been mentioned, there's an added dynamic. Mary and Joseph's family were seen as conceiving Jesus out of wedlock. And Jesus was considered illegitimate.

Israel, the Tibet of Rome

The political situation in ancient Palestine around the time of Jesus is another thing we cannot avoid discussing. Judea was basically a colonized province of Rome. The Roman Empire dictated and ruled over the Holy Land through a local king based in Jerusalem. During the earliest years of Jesus' life, that king was Herod the Great. Later, Rome replaced the king of Judea with a puppet-governor. The governor when Jesus was crucified was none other than Pontius Pilate.

Whether it was a king or a governor, they were both puppets of Rome. As historian L. Michael White puts it, "everyone knew that Rome was the power behind [it all]. Everyone knew that Rome was the source of both the wealth and also the source of some of the problems that occurred in the Jewish state. So the political reality of the day was of a dominant power overseeing the life on a day-to-day basis."[2]

No one likes to be tyrannized or oppressed. And Judea was just that—subjugated by a tyrannical and oppressive government from top to bottom. Cities like Jerusalem certainly suffered, though not as much as Nazareth. The wealth of a thriving city covers over a lot of disorder and abuse of power. Places like Nazareth, on the other hand, felt the full force of Roman occupation and oppression and its pain, humiliation, and hardship. Jesus felt it on a daily basis.

In other words, Israel was the Tibet to China's Rome. And Jesus grows up and eventually claims himself the Anointed One, akin to the Dalai Lama of Israel. He garnered followers though the religious authorities did not see him as the real "Israeli Dalai Lama."

Jesus' approach to struggling against Rome was to nonviolently fight and resist the powers that be, all the while building the commonwealth in the spirit of the people. This nonviolent fight and resistance would lead all the way to a Roman cross.

Jesus, the Mustard Plant

Jesus was like his fellow Nazarenes—living a hardscrabble life, one they all were forced to live. Unlike many of his fellow Nazarenes, Jesus encountered the judgment of his neighbors and knew the sting of rejection.

---

2. White, "Roman Empire and Judea."

Jesus once shared with his listeners a parable that most Christians know. It is the parable of the mustard seed. It goes like this:

> The kingdom of heaven is like a mustard seed that someone took and sowed in his field; it is the smallest of all the seeds, but when it has grown it is the greatest of shrubs and becomes a tree, so that the birds of the air come and make nests in its branches. (Mark 4:31–32)

Jesus, born in Bethlehem and raised in Nazareth, became a living, breathing example of a mustard seed, a divine mustard seed that grows into his anointing, changing the world all along the way.

— 5 —

Holding Cosmic Peace

> There was a man in Jerusalem whose name was Symeon, and this was a man upright and pious, eagerly awaiting the consolation of Israel, and a Holy Spirit was upon him; And it had been made known to him by the Holy Spirit that he would not die before he should see the Anointed of the Lord. And he came in the Spirit into the temple; and as the parents brought in the little child Jesus, so that they could do for him what was customary according to the Law, He took him in his arms and blessed God and said, "Now you release your servant in peace, Master, in keeping with your word; For my eyes have seen your salvation, which you have made ready before the face of all peoples, A light for a revelation to the gentiles and a glory for your people Israel. (Luke 2:25–32)

SYMEON is an old man who doesn't want to die until he sees the Anointed One, the "consolation" of his people. He is holding out hope till the very end. Why?

Luke tells us he was an upright and pious man. Heaven seems already his. Hope for heaven doesn't seem necessary, at least not for himself.

Symeon has been waiting for salvation for his people. But not just for *his* people—for *all* people. As he holds the child, he says the prayer he has been waiting to say all his life: "my eyes have seen your salvation, which you have made ready before the face of all peoples, A light for a revelation to the gentiles and a glory for your people Israel."

Imminent Salvation

Salvation is in that child right then and there. Jesus will not be *made* ready. To use a playground cliché, Jesus was born ready. As an infant, he is *already* ready, and for all peoples, both Gentile and Jew. Symeon is not pleading to somehow stick around for thirty-three more years until the day when Jesus dies on the cross or is resurrected. Salvation doesn't have to wait till then. The incarnation is enough.

And the process of holding the child provides its own quiet theophany, an experience of God amid the twilight of his years. In holding the baby Jesus, Symeon holds the embodiment of God's peace. In taking Jesus into his arms, Symeon takes God's peace into his heart. And in so doing, he opens his heart, making it capable of awakening to God's unmediated presence. Symeon's act of tenderness, the act of holding a child in his arms, removes the veil between himself and God.

The Holy Spirit, Heart-Softener

What leads *us* to this kind of theophany, this kind of God-reception? Our text from Luke mentions the Holy Spirit three times. First, the Spirit has guided Symeon's life in general. Secondly, the Holy Spirit reveals to Symeon that his death would not occur until the Anointed One came. Lastly, the Spirit leads Symeon to the temple to meet the infant Jesus.

As Symeon realized, there is a spark of the good in us, sacredly and holily moving within. If we are indeed seriously seeking truth, something will guide us on the right path to that truth. Something tenderizes the heart and makes us ready to receive the love of God. This something is the Holy Spirit. The Holy Spirit softens the hardened self and makes tender the callous heart so we can see and feel love knocking at that heart's temple door.

If we hone in on the essential process of the heart, we allow the heart to become tender and softer. And out of that tenderness and softness, receive and hold God's gift of love to us.

Context Matters

The Jewish context makes the story much clearer. According to Mosaic law, a mother was seen as needing purification after bearing a boy, even the Anointed One. This purification process took place thirty-three days after circumcision. And circumcision happened on the eighth day after birth. So, after forty-one days (thirty-three plus eight), a ritual offering could be performed. This ritual offering in effect enabled the child to be presented to the temple community and to the God worshipped therein.

Also involved in this process was a kind of tithe or tax. That tithe or tax was five shekels, the text tells us, and it was mandated by Hebrew law when presenting a baby boy to the temple.

Two turtledoves? Well, if you couldn't afford to offer a lamb, turtledoves or pigeons would suffice. This tells us that the family coming into the temple are not of the means to afford a lamb. Concisely put, this is a family dealing with some issues of poverty. Yet they are faithful whatever the costs.

We meet Jesus at forty-one days old. He is being carried by Mary and Joseph who come to the temple to present Jesus as a child of Yahweh. They come with five shekels and two turtle doves for the sacrificial offering. This was how it was done for faithful followers of Torah, the way of God.

Symeon's subsequent prophecy is likewise entrenched in Jewish tradition. It is a prophecy born of a long wait. Symeon speaks his truth to Mary. "This child is destined for the falling and the rising of many in Israel, and to be a sign that will be opposed so that the inner thoughts of many will be revealed—and a sword will pierce your own soul."

The newborn revelation that baby Jesus presents amounts to scandalous good news. He will later embody it on the cross. The good news: the kingdom of God is a revolution of the heart. It is a revolution that requires the heart be made vulnerable, that the heart be pierced and broken, in turn enabling compassion.

Messiah as Anointed Truth

In John chapter 1 we are offered the poetic version of the Christmas story. "The Word became flesh and dwelt among us." I'll offer a paraphrase that makes more sense to me. "The Word became embodied and dwelt among us." Or we might say, "The Word became a living poem."

Infant Jesus, a single-word sacred poem embodied, dwelling here and now, among us and hopefully within us—that is the meaning of Christmas for me.

As for Symeon, he holds that embodied Word in his arms. He holds that sacred poem and peers into the eyes of God.

What does the poetic truth embodied in forty-one-day-old Jesus mean? What does the Word embodied in Jesus say?

Those poor in spirit, those who've emptied themselves of go-it-aloneness, who've opened their hearts to the tenderizing power of the Spirit, who've received the impoverished power of Love, those like Symeon, will know the kingdom of heaven.

Holding-a-Baby Enlightenment

Most all of us have held a baby. Holding a baby is what peace looks like. How can you demonize, how can you hate and harm a baby or someone whose baby you hold? If enemies openheartedly held the babies of their enemies, war would cease, and peace commence.

What does it take to hold a baby? It takes a receptive, easygoing heart not afraid of being vulnerable.

To hold peace in our hearts, both externally and internally, takes the same. It takes a receptive heart toward God, others, and ourselves. A receptive heart gives way to a vulnerability that reaches out with relaxed arms and with an at-easeness capable of holding close God's gift of love.

Symeon, in holding the Prince of Peace, is assured of the world's salvation and can go and depart in peace. The world has been made right. May we sit and hold peace in our arms. May we internalize peace and breathe that peace into the world. May we know the enlightenment of holding the infant Jesus in our arms and seeing the universal light of salvation.

— 6 —

Nativity's Interreligious Event

I REMEMBER a weekly ritual I had for a summer or two when I was ten or eleven years old. On late weekday afternoons, once a week, I would walk from our apartment a few blocks over to Warren Street, Hudson's main street. I would walk up Warren to Hudson Diner, a traditional metal boxcar diner. It is still there. I'd get a cheeseburger, fries, and a chocolate milk. I'd order, eat, and pay for it, proud of my burgeoning sense of independence and freedom. I hope I was smart enough to leave a tip.

I'd finish and walk a couple blocks down Warren to the corner of 5th Street and wait for the bus, my dad's bus returning from his commuter line run to Albany. His line run done, he would be heading back to the bus depot to finish his day. I'd catch the bus just to hang out with him.

I'd get on, the bus empty. As I looked on admiringly, he'd drive the big coach out of Hudson, across the Rip Van Winkle Bridge to Coxsackie, where the depot was. Those twenty-to-thirty minutes, framed by lingering cigarette smoke and diesel fumes, snippets of father-son conversation and the surrounding silence, filled my spirit.

We'd arrive at the depot and he'd do his paper work and chat and joke around with some of his colleagues. I was proud to be seen for what I was—Donnie's son. I think my dad too was proud to have me there. After finishing his day, we'd get in his '75 Ford Maverick and head back home, the difference between the car and the bus striking to me. And we'd reach home, though home was with me the whole time.

Where the Heart Is

Christmas is the season full of images, thoughts, and lyrics of home. "I'll be home for Christmas." "There's no place like home for the holidays." "Please come home for Christmas." The movie *A Christmas Story* is replete with memories of home. And then there are the *Home Alone* movies.

The original story, the Nativity story, also includes themes of home. The story of Jesus' birth is full of journeys toward home. Jesus is born not in his hometown, Nazareth, but in Bethlehem. He must return home.

After Jesus' birth, parents and child sojourn back to Nazareth. There is a significant detour on that journey home. The holy family must flee to Egypt, refugees to escape Herod's evil plans. Eventually they return home to Nazareth. Imagine their feelings upon returning home after their long ordeal as refugees so far from the shelter of home.

Sages Leave Home

There is another story in the birth narrative about a journey away from home and back. This one involves key characters in Nativity crèches everywhere—the Magi, sometimes called "the Wisemen" or even "the Sages." I will refer to them as the Sages.

It is not clear where these Sages were from. It's not even clear how many there were. In crèches and manger scenes everywhere, there are usually three. But the biblical text doesn't indicate the number. As for where they came from, scholars believe they came from possibly Persia or India, or maybe as far east as Mongolia.

They leave home, following the star to what they believe is a new hope. They are brought to Jerusalem and to King Herod, who in turn sends them forth as spies to find the location of Jesus. The implication is that Herod wants to get rid of this infant threat. They are to find Jesus and then return to Jerusalem to report back to Herod the babe king's destination.

The Sages follow the star further west. They most certainly traveled via the Silk Road, the ancient trading route going from China to Greece with stops near Jerusalem. The star eventually brings them to Jesus, now in Nazareth at home. The Sages were not at the manger in Bethlehem. The Sages visit a toddler-aged Jesus at home in Nazareth.

As they visit Jesus, they realize they are looking at something divine. Matthew 2 says they saw the child with his mother Mary and fell to the ground and prostrated before the child in reverence. They presented him with precious gifts—gold, frankincense, and myrrh.

Gentile Sages, Growing Faith

Now, it is clear the Sages were not Jewish. They were Gentiles, maybe Zoroastrians, maybe Hindus or even Buddhists. Whatever their faith was, they did not share Joseph and Mary's Yahweh-Torah faith. And whatever their faith, they and their faith were transformed in some way as they adoringly experienced the presence of the child.

I imagine being so far from home after many months of travel, they longed for home. And in this beautiful child, they sensed something profoundly welcoming and homelike. They felt welcomed, embraced, accepted just as they were. The child and the presence of the child did not exclude them in anyway. Like all holy experiences, this holy experience recalled home, the home they were hundreds and hundreds of miles away from, the home that gave them meaning, purpose, and belonging.

That said, there's no mention in the story of the Sages converting to Judaism after meeting this newborn said to be the Jewish messiah. The Sages never call the young Jesus "Lord" or "Messiah." They are personally transformed but the transformation is not to a new religion per se.

Instead of conversion to a new religion, they are transformed to a newer, deeper way of living their own respective faiths. They return home changed in the wake of it all, renewed by that moment with the holy child, a moment that never leaves them. A little bit lighter and uplifted, they return to live their faiths in their own cultural home. We can safely assume they practice their faiths for the rest of their days.

— 7 —

The First Carol

The Jesus Hymn

*Let the same mind be in you
that was in Christ Jesus, who,
though he was in the image of God,
did not regard equality with God
as something to be exploited,
but emptied himself,
taking the form of a servant,
being born in human likeness.
And being found in human form,
he humbled himself . . .*

To close out this first part of my book, I'd like to look at perhaps the earliest description of the Christmas story, the story of the Christ encountering this earth and transforming it. It is known as the Jesus Hymn. It comes from Philippians 2 and is believed to be an early Christian hymn that predates Paul's letters, which are the earliest pieces of scripture of the New Testament. And since Paul's letters predate all four Gospels, so does the Jesus Hymn. Before the Christian church had a New Testament, they had this hymn. Anyway, let us focus in on the Christmas story portion of the text.

The nature of Jesus' divinity is not my focus here. What is done with innate divinity, with "image of God" nature, is the focus.

The Jesus Hymn seems to say even though Jesus is fully the image of God, he did not seek to possess equality with God, nor did he exploit his "image of God" nature for self-gain. His sacredness was not taken advantage of nor lauded over others. But it was given away and emptied.

Why? Because help is needed, because humankind needs transformation, needs enlightenment, needs salvation, needs love. The divine idea is "Just because I am divine doesn't mean I should just remain content here in heaven, loving life and all its luxuries when people on earth need me."

And so, the Word became flesh and dwelt among us, as John 1 says. Our text in Philippians says Christ emptied himself. He let go of his claim to divinity to be with us and to help us find our way. To help humanity, God, through Christ, is embodied in the lowliest human form—a servant, a slave. This embodiment is known in Christianity as the incarnation.

Interfaith Incarnation

I should say here that this idea of incarnation is not novel or unique to Christianity. Buddhism, for example, has a similar concept in its teaching on the bodhisattva. The bodhisattva is a fully enlightened being that is equal in essence to a Buddha, or we might say is divine. An infinite freedom in the heaven of Nirvana is due the bodhisattva. An existence of complete contentment and perfection apart from this world is his or hers. But the bodhisattva hears the cries and suffering and angst of the world and cannot turn away. The bodhisattva in turn takes on the form of a sentient being. The bodhisattva incarnates human form to save others. The bodhisattva empties him or herself and returns to the world of suffering and pain to bring others to enlightenment, transformation, salvation.

Judaism also has within it some kind of understanding of incarnation, at least of God appearing on earth to show humans something integral. In the Hebrew scriptures, there is the frequent appearance of the angel of the Lord. The most famous appearance comes in the famous fiery bush scene where the angel of the Lord appears in the fiery bush and says, "I am the God of your father, the God of Abraham, the God of Isaac, and the God of Jacob." Traditional Christian interpreters of the Hebrew scriptures claim that whenever there are appearances of the angel of the Lord in the Hebrew text, we have pre-Jesus examples of temporary incarnation. Jews simply see it as examples of theophanies, God-epiphanies, or examples of humans experiencing God here on earth.

Humility, Humanity, and Holiness

What is astounding to me is the form that the appearance of God takes according to Philippians. God empties himself of the highest form we know, that of divinity, that of perfect and complete holiness, and takes on the form of a servant. God, perfect and divine, becomes a nobody in the world's eyes, becomes a servant to save us. This at once humbles divinity and reifies the nobodies among us.

God is shown to us most fully by being born to us, born in the same way any baby is born. God becomes a baby wrapped in swaddling clothes.

I've attended one birth—the birth of my son. I can tell you there is nothing as humble or as humbling, nor as sacred and holy, as the birth of a child. In the act of a baby being born resides the whole story of humanity and divinity dwelling together, of the profane and the sacred in perfect harmony.

And in the presence of the child born in a stable and set in a feeding trough, we have a picture, a living portrait of God here and now. God takes on the lowliest of places and in so doing points to the sacred therein. It is one thing for God to appear in the form of an angel as he does in the Hebrew scriptures. But here God appears in the painful and earthy process of childbirth, which takes place not in a sanitized hospital room or bedroom, but in a barn. For God to visit us in the breath of a newborn baby screaming into the world—what an amazing thing.

So, there we go. That is what Christmas is all about, Charlie Brown.

Herodly Power vs. Godly Power

The juxtaposition between what Herod does in Matthew 2[1] and what God does in Philippians 2 is telling and gives us an important teaching of Christmas wisdom.

Whereas God empties himself, the Herods among us are full of themselves. Whereas sovereign God takes on the form of a servant, Herods do everything to maintain their false sovereignty. Whereas God humbles

---

1. To remove baby Jesus, seen as a threat to his power, Herod, as the story goes, issues the "slaughter of innocence" where boys under the age of two in and around Bethlehem are killed. Historians doubt the historicity of this event and suggest it is meant to mirror Pharaoh's similar act in Exodus. Because of a dream telling Joseph to flee to Egypt, Jesus is spared.

himself, Herods marinate in pride and anger. Whereas God is born in human form, Herods seek to discard and dismiss the vulnerable.

We are called to be of the same mind as in Christ Jesus, who emptied himself, who became a lowly servant, who humbled himself, who was born as a helpless child. But we too often play the part of Herod, at least in our hearts. We are too full of ourselves. We are too wrapped up in our power and riches and our desire for things. We are too proud and angry and selfish. We are too cavalier and careless when it comes to the preciousness of each and every child and each and every breath.

No More Strawmen

These silly strawmen that shout on cable news about the war on Christmas don't get it. The noise that says we are removing the reason for the season, that we are killing Christmas, ignores the point. These simplistic annual forays into meaningless chatter mask and hide the real story.

This is the real story: The way to really live out the true meaning of Christmas is to love Jesus by loving and protecting our children and all of God's children. How? By emptying ourselves of our ego, our power-hungriness, our soul-killing greed and human-killing weapons, and out of this emptiness and humility, being spiritually born again in baby Jesus and in each and every child's breath. Let it all go, and lose ourselves in the God of all things, in Emmanuel, God-with-us.

We are called to be of the same mind as the divine infant lying in the manger. If this state of mind is realized, everything will be different.

Part 2

The Compassion of the Passion

— 8 —

Cleansing the Temple Sunday

It all begins with a processional. It begins with Jesus entering Jerusalem for the specific purpose of telling the truth and pointing to the heart of the matter. The truth remains. The powers of the world torture the spirit, degrade life, making it seem dead, making it impossible for the poor and for the already hurting. Jesus goes to tell the truth despite the consequences, consequences he knew were grave.

Jesus straddles a donkey and marches into Jerusalem with a heavy heart. We often forget that Jesus is grieving for most of his three-year ministry. He is grieving the loss of his cousin and his spiritual mentor, the person who baptized him, the person who paved the way to the truth and the life Jesus would offer. John the Baptist was martyred merely one to two years prior to what we know now as Palm Sunday.

Jesus also almost lost his friend Lazarus. "He wept" as he internalized the sadness. Jesus comes into Jerusalem to face the same fate as John and Lazarus.

Jesus also felt and carried with him the suffering of his people—the diseased, the sick, the socially isolated and excluded, the discarded all around him. He grieves the spiritual and emotional loss all around him.

This sorrow has not disappeared. Jesus carries all this sorrow as he marches into Jerusalem. Despite the glory and praise thrown at him, despite the lovely palms on the road into Jerusalem and the accompanying shouts of hosannas, Jesus is grieving loss, a lot of it. We have in Jesus entering Jerusalem "a man of constant sorrow," as Bluegrass legend Ralph Stanley once sang. And as Handel wrote in another, much older masterpiece, *Messiah*, Jesus was "a man of sorrows and acquainted with grief."

March on Jerusalem

The man of constant sorrow, despite the sorrow, is coming into Jerusalem. His sorrow will soon reveal a righteous anger and a righteous cause.

Jesus' very entrance was a political act. We can call it the March on Jerusalem. He was entering like a royal but riding on a donkey. Those who ride on a donkey in a royal procession make a clear statement. Jesus proclaims without a word, "I come in peace and humility."

Those who ride in on horses, such as Roman emperors or their handmaiden governors, come declaring dominance, control, and war if need be. Juxtaposing himself to this, Jesus declares himself the bringer of a new way of doing kingdom. Jesus arrives offering a commonwealth led by a Father's love.

Studied Jews would also know the scripture in Zechariah pointing to a new king arriving and riding on a humble beast of burden, a working animal. They knew the significance and the courage of doing so in the face of Roman oppression. To the Roman Empire, this was indeed a direct threat to its power.

This new king was an anti-king, riding not in majesty but in humility. He was giving a most powerful speech by just riding in. He preaches against the corrupt, prideful powers with each and every marching step into Jerusalem.

Occupy the Temple

A powerful wind of change moves Jesus forward. His political act, his coming into Jerusalem as the anti-king facilitator of God's commonwealth, was followed by a more pointed political act.

The temple cleansing that follows is not a crime of passion. Jesus didn't come riding into Jerusalem ignorant of what he'd find there. He has seen Jerusalem many times. He came to the temple at Passover every year as did every faithful Yahweh-Torah follower. Each year he has seen the temple at Passover time, a time ripe with corruption and moneymaking schemes. The moneychangers and merchants were not a new thing.

Cleansing the Temple Sunday

Jesus' Palm Sunday actions are premeditated. When he arrives, he does not impulsively lose his cool and yell people out of the temple. Jesus comes into Jerusalem to do exactly what he eventually does. It was a preplanned act of civil disobedience, declaring that all was not right, that a loving God needed to be enthroned in both the temple and in the hearts of the people suffering through occupation and oppression.

This close-to-violent protest—the closest Jesus ever came to being violent—was meant for the religious side of power's abuse, the temple hierarchy. He matches the spiritual violence of mixing greed and faith with the physical violence of overturning tables and running greed out of the temple.

Jesus cleanses the temple because it has come to mirror the Empire instead of spiritually counteracting it. Jesus proclaims that God's commonwealth confronts and overturns old, corrupt ways of doing things, transforming what it confronts into the likeness of God, in the likeness of Love. Neither secular power nor religious power would be spared the force of Love, whose power derives from its heart of vulnerable compassion.

Sorrow Expected but Still Surprising

Still, though his act was planned, the sight of the temple at Passover still hurt, still hit him deep and dark. You can hear your best friend is really ill in the hospital, drive hours to visit, and imagine what you will see yet still be devastated by what you see when you arrive. Injustice and greed and unrighteousness can shock us even when we've come to expect it. Jesus is confronted again by the reality of the temple's failure and fallenness.

He comes into Jerusalem a man of constant sorrow. More sorrow awaits. Jesus' own self is confronted by the temple's failure and fallenness. Each year profit was being made at the temple, mostly on the backs of poor people who were mandated to buy sacrifices to offer at Passover. It's not just that the moneychangers buy and sell things. They sell animals to be sacrificed and offered at Passover and price-gouge the people. This effects the poor most acutely. The moneychangers and merchants are robbing the poor, especially widows and women, who were at a particular disadvantage in the schemes to sell cheap sacrifices, like doves, offered at Passover.

Jesus could not help but to take it deeply personally. The earthly center of his faith was this temple in Jerusalem. Each time he visited the temple, he faced the reality that this place he held so dear in his heart was helplessly corrupt and unrighteous. Pain pivoted to anger. This time anger would spill over.

So, the Lamb becomes a lioness protecting the vulnerable, the poor, the ignored, the marginalized continually deprived of the spiritual nutrient of a pure faith and the compassion of a helping hand.

> Jesus entered the temple courts and began driving out those who were buying and selling there. He overturned the tables of the money changers and the benches of those selling doves, and would not allow anyone to carry merchandise through the temple courts. And as he taught them, he said, "Is it not written: 'My house will be called a house of prayer for all nations'? But you have made it 'a den of robbers.'" (Mark 11:15–18, NIV)

Cleanse the Church Sunday

It's interesting to me, though not all that surprising, that for the institutional church the palms and praises are primary and most prominent in our remembrance of this part of Jesus' story. Jesus' majestic arrival into Jerusalem stands so prominent that it has its own Sunday, Palm Sunday. It's as if we want to glorify the king yet forget the prophet.

Why is the story of Jesus' cleansing of the temple made to be secondary? As the church developed and became more like the temple that Jesus confronted, the palms, the praises, and the pomp and circumstance became most prominent. The cleansing of the temple, while more pertinent to the church than the palms and the praise, is relegated to the lectionary.

The church in many ways is the temple that Jesus rode on a palm-covered road to make right. While it is true that neither the Protestant nor the Catholic Church is as dominant or as rich as they used to be, they still stake their claim to fame and importance. Churches are closing all around us, but we still cling to a worldly idea of power. We cling to hierarchy, to memories of importance and history, to the way things have always been done. We cling to these habits instead of letting them go enough to transform us.

How different things would be if on Palm Sunday we commemorated a cleansing of all that holds church communities back. How different things would be if, along with the palms taken home, we took into our hearts a renewed dedication to live in the way of radical love as Christ's disciples and church.

Cleansing the Temple Sunday

Yes, it is good to welcome Jesus with palms and praise. It is good to welcome him and his way of love with an open heart. But don't forget the cleansing, the cleansing away of all that holds us back.

Maybe one day the palms will become a symbol not of merely the kingly glory of the march into Jerusalem but of something far more applicable. Maybe one day it will be a symbol of receiving Jesus' way of self-emptying compassion into our hearts, a reception that in turn cleanses our hearts of all that holds us as a community and as a society back.

— 9 —

Extremist in the Offense of Liberation

In the Palm Sunday story, we see Jesus' humility clearly. Here he is, a king, riding into Jerusalem not in a limousine of the best horses and a coach of gold, nor with a banner declaring greatness or a hat about greatness and victory. Jesus comes not with speeches embodying strength and winning. No, Jesus rides into Jerusalem on a donkey, and does so silently.

There are shouts of hosanna all around him. However, Jesus knows he goes to Jerusalem to be condemned. And this is the point of his going. He goes into Jerusalem not to win in the eyes of the world. He goes into Jerusalem to lose in the eyes of a win-at-all-cost world. He goes into Jerusalem to accept defeat, a deadly defeat. He will lose in the world's eyes to change that world's heart.

Later, after that donkey ride into Jerusalem, we see Jesus and his disciples at Passover. During the meal, he points directly at extreme humility. We read in John 13 about Jesus' act of utter servanthood, an act that foreshadows a greater, more brutal act to come, that of dying on the cross.

Liberation Leadership

Jesus in this act of washing his disciples' feet defines godly leadership for us. He also defines liberation. Liberation and the liberator infuse humility and compassion.

> He poured water into a basin and began to wash his disciples' feet, drying them with the towel that was wrapped around him.

Extremist in the Offense of Liberation

> When he had finished washing their feet, he put on his clothes and returned to his place. "Do you understand what I have done for you?" he asked them. "You call me 'Teacher' and 'Master,' and rightly so, for that is what I am. Now that I, your Master and Teacher, have washed your feet, you also should wash one another's feet. I have set you an example that you should do as I have done for you. Very truly I tell you, no servant is greater than his master, nor is a messenger greater than the one who sent him. Now that you know these things, you will be blessed if you do them. (John 13:5, 12–17)

Jesus in this act embodies humility and service as a servant. This is not just verbalized humility or service or servanthood. This simple yet profound and powerful act is in many Christian traditions a sacramental act. From Primitive Baptists in Appalachia to Eastern Orthodox Christians in Albania, we see foot-washing ceremonies occurring.

The Church of the Brethren, part of the Anabaptist and Peace Church movement, combines Communion and a foot-washing ceremony together. It is termed "the Love Feast." It is a practice that occurs monthly usually.

Some traditions memorialize the foot washing ceremony on Maundy Thursday. Pope Francis has made an annual practice of going to a prison or a homeless shelter or a mosque to portray in ritualized form what it means to humble oneself and serve another.

With the humble now iconic act, Jesus shows us the heart of community. Without such radical humility, a community always risks becoming a battle of big egos. Without such radical humility, things too easily become a battle between power-hungry competitors. In this battle, the so-called fittest survive by preying on the vulnerable.

Radical humility, especially when applied and practiced by the powerful, removes the danger of such power plays. Radical humility, as *personified* in Jesus, allows the powerful to truly see the less powerful and the powerless.

I will have more to say about Jesus' iconic act in the next chapter.

Extremist Jesus

This figure Jesus of Nazareth is not to be ignored. Preaching and practicing radical humility, Jesus is pushing buttons. He is getting under the skin of just about everyone. He is stirring trouble. He is, as civil rights hero and icon John Lewis urges, getting in the way.

Why? Why is this unordained, unofficial religious teacher from the backwoods of Nazareth such a thorn in the side of the powers that be? What is it about him that disturbs the establishment and garners so much support from the common people?

Have you ever noticed that extremes disturb some yet also attract others? Barry Goldwater in 1968 offered us some rather infamous words. He said, "extremism in the defense of liberty is no vice." Folks cheered then. Folks cheer now.

Was Jesus extreme in defense of liberty? There are a few questions packed in that one question, actually.

Was Jesus extreme? If so, what was the nature of his extremism?

And was he defending liberty? If not, what was his point?

First of all, we must be honest; Jesus *was* extreme. He was an extremist. Only an extremist could garner so much angst, so much hatred, so much resistance. The religious and political powers agreed that Jesus was too extreme to ignore. In fact, he was too extreme to keep around.

But we must ask the next question: What was the nature of Jesus' extremism? What was he extreme about? As Dr. Martin Luther King Jr. once reminded us, Jesus was an extremist for love.[1]

He was, first of all, extreme in his definition of God. To Jesus, God is a Father who embraces all, who finds all those left behind, all those who are excluded, even those who've excluded themselves.

Not only this, Jesus himself was extreme in his humility. This makes sense. There is a connection between love and humility. We know this in our relationships. If love is to last, if love is to live, if love is to win, those who love must profoundly practice humility. Pride and selfishness are the enemy of love. Humility and selflessness are love's nourishment.

Jesus' love for people was based on his selflessness and his humility. Jesus' work—from his humble birth and childhood to his three-year-long healing and teaching ministry to his week-long passion story—was based on his selflessness and humility.

Liberation on Offense

So, Jesus was an extremist for love and selflessness. That much is clear. Was he defending liberty with his extremism?

---

1. Dr. King wrote, "Jesus Christ was an extremist for love truth and goodness, and thereby rose above his environment." King, "Letter from a Birmingham Jail,", 289.

If we change that word "defend" to "offend," and if we change the word "liberty" to "liberation," we come up with a more apt description of Jesus' *raison d'etre*. Jesus' extremism was in the offense of liberation.

Jesus was not defending anything. There was nothing to defend. What he was offering didn't exist. He was offering spiritual liberation that led to complete, collective liberation. He was going on the offense. Jesus had the ball and he was aiming for the liberation of all.

He marched down the field and into Jerusalem to win all peoples' liberation, beginning with the least, the lost, the losers in the world's eyes, beginning with those imprisoned and oppressed. And at the foundation of this gospel of liberation is love and compassion born of God. At the heart of this liberation is a love so extreme that it gives self away and embodies true self at the same time.

Offense's Double Entendre

In English, the word "offense" has a double meaning. Offense can mean the opposite of defense, as in the best offense is a good defense. Or it can be related to offending or being offended, as in "she took offense to my sermon."

Jesus uses ultimate love as his offense in the former sense—as opposite of defense—to defeat oppression and win us liberation. But this offense of radical love, in our world, is offensive to many, isn't it? The love and humility Jesus radically offered still offends. The Gospel of Mark tells us how Jesus was scandalous to the self-righteous and self-important. Mark 6:3 says, "They were deeply offended about Jesus and they refused to believe in Him." The word translated "deeply offended" is *scandalon*, from which we get "scandalous."

Scandal with a Purpose

As our culture and times show, anyone can be scandalous. Anyone can be offensive with their words or deeds. The question is what is the point? What is the goal? What is the purpose of such offensive actions?

For Jesus, his offense to win liberation and his offense, his scandal, were one and the same. Jesus' means and ends matched. The aim, the goal, the end, was a liberating love, and the means he used to get there was liberating love. The offense he used to get us down the field and what offended so many in the process was one and the same—he loved the most excluded, the marginalized, the oppressed equally and walked with them, talked with them, served them, died in their place. Love, and the liberation love naturally brings, was Jesus' divine aim and divine way.

I close with a Christian paraphrase of Goldwater—extreme love in the offense of liberation is Christian. In other words, as it was with Jesus, let God's radical love be the benchmark in all we do, including in who we want to lead us.

— 10 —

Passion and Transmitted-Salvation

I REMEMBER having a conversation with a Korean student in a Conversational English class I was teaching while in Korea. She was a devout Christian. Our conversation was friendly but we were clear about our differences. She was adamant about Christ's uniqueness. I resisted ultimate uniqueness in Jesus alone, seeing uniqueness in other religious figures, namely for me the Buddha. During our discussion, the student asked me a question, a really probing one. She asked, "Jesus died on the cross for others; what did the Buddha do that was as great?"

I've been sitting with that question for years. I've come to see that indeed Jesus was unique. While he didn't teach for sixty years like the Buddha, he was committed to nonviolence and to his disciples in a unique and unparalleled way. And he used nonviolence to protect his disciples, dying to protect them amid the conflict and chaos surrounding his arrest in Jerusalem. He, the Good Shepherd, died protecting his sheep.

In other words, Jesus practiced what he preached to the bitter end. He perfectly lived out the love he pointed to. He embodied that love. His life and death were living scriptures exemplifying the good news he revealed. Christ's uniqueness resides in the extent to which he embodied self-emptying compassion—all the way to the cross.

In many ways, I am getting to the heart of this book and to my understanding of Jesus and his work, namely his death. Jesus' death was his teaching lived out completely.

Substituting Substitution

The traditional view of Christ's death is that Christ died for humankind, in all of humanity's place, for the world's sins and for the wages of the world's sins, which is death. The fancy theological term for this is "substitutiary atonement." As the idea goes, each of us are deserving of spiritual lifelessness and suffering because of our fallen state. But Jesus became humanity's substitute on the cross. And through his being our substitute, we are atoned, put right in the eyes of God.

I want to offer an alternative view. It is an alternative view that takes the crucifixion as absolutely pivotal to the Jesus story and to the church in his name. Yet it is a view that does not theologize away the historical event of Jesus' crucifixion. I am calling it the "transmitted-substitutiary atonement model." To see what I am getting at we must go back to the first-century Roman Empire.

Once Again, Context Matters

Jesus is the leader of a radical Jewish movement in the context of Roman occupation of the Holy Land. After about three years of teaching and stirring controversy, Jesus enters Jerusalem, where he kicks the controversy into high gear. He does this by ransacking the temple and running the fundraisers and moneychangers out of the temple. This offends the religious authorities in charge of the temple.

The controversy whirling around Jesus eventually makes its way to the ears of the Roman authorities in the area. It now reaches a level where not only Jesus but also his close band of disciples are in danger of arrest and penalty.

What's more, the authorities do not have a clue, nor care to, about the nature of Jesus' teaching and its call to peace and love. Aggressive rebellion was in the air and the word on the street. Was Jesus leading a rebellion? To the authorities the answer seemed to be yes. What's more, based on the physicality of Jesus' work in the temple, it could easily be assumed that Jesus' rebellion was aggressive and violent.

All of this is to say, the authorities are out to get Jesus and his disciples. They are out to end this rebellion before it gets started no matter what it takes.

Jesus had two choices: fight Rome or flee Rome. Completely fleeing wasn't an option. Jesus had been preaching the commonwealth of God since the start. Preaching about it without trying to build it was not the Jesus way. He was, after all, anointed to "preach good news to the poor . . . proclaim deliverance to the captives and recovery of sight to the blind, to release the oppressed, to proclaim the year of the Lord's favor." He had come to Jerusalem for this purpose.

Fighting Rome was also not an option, at least not in the way Rome fought. Fighting like Rome—i.e., violently—would mean sure defeat. And it would be a deadly defeat. It would mean not only violence but death for many if not all of his disciples and followers. This would mean the death of Christ's dream of God's commonwealth. The dream would die with he and his disciples in battle.

The only valid, life-affirming choice was this: Jesus would choose to fight, but nonviolently by giving himself up in an act of civil disobedience. He'd have his disciples flee to continue with the struggle. He'd leave his disciples to continue in the building of the commonwealth, knowing someday even Rome would capitulate.

The First Lord's Supper

We come to the event that begins the climax of the Jesus story. That event is a meal, a festive feast known as the Passover meal. With this meal Christianity's key liturgical practice is initiated. Some, like myself, call it Communion. Some call it Lord's Supper. Some call it Eucharist. Some consider it a sacrament. Some call it a symbolic practice. Regardless of how one sees it, the practice of Communion connects practitioners back to Jesus and his first disciples.

Communion as introduced in scripture shows something very revealing. It shows us that Jesus' pending sacrificial death was limited in its purpose, focused on his disciples and his band of followers and their salvation.

Jesus introduces the practice of Communion *to* his disciples, *for* his disciples. This becomes clear in looking at the four versions of Jesus introducing Communion, the first Communion.

The Communion practice, as most who attend church know, is the practice of partaking of the wafer or bread and wine or juice with the mindset that the elements represent Christ's body and blood. Protestant churches see it as either a sacrament or a remembrance that holds special spiritual resonance. Catholic churches see it as a sacrament and even more spiritually pertinent. We'll leave the discussion of the difference between Protestant understandings and the Catholic understanding alone. The focus here is whom that first Communion meal was for.

The Four Renderings

As noted, four renderings of that first Communion exist.[1] The earliest rendering appears in Paul's First Letter to the Corinthians some twenty years following Christ's departure. Paul states the Lord appeared to him and informed him of that original event with Jesus and his disciples at Passover meal. In Paul's telling, Jesus is speaking to his disciples. He passes unleavened, flat bread and says, "This is my body broken *for you.*"

That "for you" is important in our discussion. Jesus says, "My body, soon to be broken, will be for *you*, for you my disciples." Jesus then passes wine and indicates that the wine represents the new covenant offered by his lifeblood. While Jesus doesn't parallel things by saying the blood poured out is likewise just "for you," that is the implication.

Luke's later rendering of that first Communion also makes clear that Jesus is speaking with his disciples and that he says to them that both the body broken and the blood poured out is "for you." Jesus states, "The sacrifice to come is for you, on behalf of you, my disciples."

As for Mark and Matthew, the other two renderings, there is some variance. Mark, like Paul's First Letter to the Corinthians and Luke's Gospel, has Jesus speaking to his disciples at Passover. However, Mark quotes Jesus as saying "the blood of the covenant poured out *for many.*" What's more, Matthew concurs with Mark when it comes to "for many" and adds *"for the remission of sins."* Interestingly, neither Matthew or Mark calls the covenant "new" like Paul does.

To summarize the four renderings, Paul's is the earliest rendering and he received this rendering from, we presume, the disciples who were there. Paul has Jesus narrowing the practice of Communion and the crucifixion it foreshadowed, being purposefully focused on his closest friends, his beloved disciples. Luke concurs with this.

Mark's rendering is next in line as far as the date of authorship goes, written after Paul's First Letter to the Corinthians and before Matthew and Luke. Mark shows Jesus speaking to his disciples as he is in Paul and Luke.

---

1. 1 Corinthians 11:23–16; Mark 14:22–25; Luke 22:14–20; Matthew 26:26–30.

But Mark expands the "for you" to "for many." Matthew concurs and adds "for remission of sins."

Matthew's intriguing add-on is not found in the other three, nor in the Gospel of John's unique reference to the body and blood as broken bread and poured wine. I think it is the author of Matthew's add-on, and not original to the first Communion.

Who Gets It Right?

"For you" and "for many" are very distinct propositions. Who is correct here? Who gets the words of Jesus correctly? It is impossible to say for sure. However, we can make some observations that help us understand what that first Communion was all about.

First of all, from the very beginning of the church there was tension about whom the Jesus movement was for. Jewish-based followers narrowed things to the disciples and those like the disciples, i.e., practicing Jews. Communion was introduced to the disciples at the Last Supper first and foremost and it was passed down by those disciples to subsequent disciples. To partake of that sacred remembrance, one had to be a Torah-follower in full, i.e., Jewish. That's what all of Paul's talk about circumcision and the Law is about, him disagreeing with this idea of Torah-following as the first mandated step to be a Jesus-follower.

Gentile followers of Jesus very soon joined the Jesus movement after his departure. By their very addition, the Gentile-followers were expanding the Jesus movement. Still, there was an early debate within the church about whether the faith was to remain particular and focused on Jewish followers of Jesus or whether the faith was to expand and become universal, offered to Jews and Gentiles alike. Paul was the leader of the movement to expand the Jesus tradition and welcome in Gentiles. Luke, a Gentile himself, naturally affirmed Paul's approach.

It is interesting that Paul, quoting the disciples who were there, maintains the particularity of the original Communion meal, affirming "for you" instead of "for many." Luke also maintains the particularity. Despite Paul and Luke's desire to universalize the Jesus movement and make it more inclusive, they both agree that Jesus at this point is speaking exclusively to his disciples.

Mark and Matthew, writing to Jews and for Jews, were also calling for an expansion, a furthering of the reach to many. (The early Jewish

Christians lose the debate and so don't really have specific authorship in the Gospels; the closest we get is the Epistle of James, written by the brother of Jesus and leader of the Jewish Christian branch). In Mark and Matthew's Gospels, they are making their argument for expansion clear and pleading their case to a people who are resistant to the idea. Matthew and Mark are saying, things have changed, the gospel is not just for you, my Jewish brothers and sisters, but for many, including Gentiles. The "for many" fits their argument.

I think Paul and Luke get the story most accurately. Their telling of the story contradicts their interest. If the Jesus movement is for whomever chooses to follow, yet the first Communion was specifically focused on the disciples, there is an internal contradiction. If you quote something that is, as Bart Ehrman states, "contrary to your own interests," yet you quote it anyway, it is far more likely that the quote is accurate. Hence, I think Paul and Luke's "for you" get at the original words.[2]

As for Mark and Matthew, they are speaking to exclusivist adherents to the Yahweh faith of Israel and arguing for an inclusivist, expansivist approach to that faith. It is in their interest to expand the narrower "for you" to a more inclusivist, expansivist "for many" and "for the forgiveness of sins."

Does a Dozen Equal Many?

The "for many" is seen by some as an idiom meaning "for all." *Polys* is Greek for "many" but can sometimes be idiomatic for "all."[3] How do we know when *polys* is to be read literally or idiomatically? In scripture, *polys* is almost always translated "many." It is unclear if *polys* here means "all."

We must ask whether "the disciples" in our story mean just the twelve apostles or mean the twelve plus the many other non-apostolic disciples Jesus had. After all, twelve is a figurative number.

Certainly, Jesus had a close-knit inner circle, sometimes called "the Twelve" or "the Apostles." But close, devout female followers of Jesus are also essential in the Gospels, e.g., Mary Magdalene. These women were also part of that inner circle.

Moreover, there were far more than just twelve to fifteen followers of Jesus. If there were just twelve to fifteen Jesus-followers, Rome and the

2. Ehrman, "How Jesus Became God," at 42:25.
3. Smail, *Once and for All*, 36; Pinnock, *Grace of God*, 59

religious hierarchy would not have been so perturbed. There were *many* followers of Jesus. These many followers were sometimes referred to generally as disciples.

So, the *polys* Jesus mentions in Mark and Matthew could mean Jesus' many disciples and not just the twelve there at the first Communion event. Mark and Matthew merely expand Communion, broadening it to include not just those who were there at the first Lord's Table but to the many followers who weren't physically there at the table.

Nonetheless, it is easy to see how a literal "many" becomes an idiomatic "all." The process of going from many to all points to the trajectory of the new Jesus faith. Jesus himself commands his disciples to preach good news to all the nations. However, he began with the nation of Israel and expanded the particular of his surroundings to the universal of all the nations. He called on the troops to continue this expanding of the net in their work of being disciples of human beings.

From Singular to Multiplicity

In the Gospel of John, Jesus makes a curious statement. He says in John 12:24–26, "Very truly I tell you, unless a kernel of wheat falls to the ground and dies, it remains only a single seed. But if it dies, it produces many seeds (NIV)." In other words, Jesus is a single seed. His crucifixion means that single seed becomes many.

The trajectory from one to many, this progressive movement from a single ripple in the water expanding outward, this is at the heart of Jesus' work, especially his work on the cross. We are not talking a universal beginning here. Jesus' death is an opening act to a never-ending play. We are talking a particular beginning with universal reach. We are talking a singularity-fueled Big Bang that leads to an expanding universal spirituality. That is what the cross represents. The cross represents human transformation's Big Bang. (We will talk about this more in chapter 5.)

Jesus said "for you." But like the singular seed of wheat that falls and leads to multiplicity, the "for you" leads to "for many." Through the select few of the inner circle, through the numerous direct disciples of Jesus, and through the church that follows, many, many more come to receive the good news of the Nazarene.

The Elect

There is still a debate going on between old-school, "Jesus died just for the elect only" Calvinists and newer-school, "Jesus died for all" Arminians. I am by no means an elect-onlyist who believes only the select-few will be saved. I am a Universalist who believes all in the end will know salvation.

However, I think Calvin sensed in scripture that Jesus in the Gospels is focused on his disciples. He is speaking to them, teaching them, guiding them, and directing them to continue in the work he has begun. And I believe he dies for them, his disciples, so this work can continue.

The Elect are Jesus' first-generation apostles and disciples, those who heard his teaching and followed him directly. Jesus is a pebble in a pond. The first ripple is the disciples that make up the Elect. The Elect move the subsequent ripples outward. These ripples, because they were first moved by the Eternal One, continue endlessly.

The first apostles and disciples are the select few (the Elect). They amount to the mustard seed Jesus once pointed to as representative of expansive faith. Something big came from a small package, if you will. We begin with the Elect, and from the Elect we get the "All in All."

Substitutiary Death for Disciples

Again, I believe Jesus dies in the stead of his disciples to shield them from Roman death. He is a substitute for the whole movement he has commenced and has been leading. He dies to keep that movement going forward, and even to kick it into high gear after he is physically gone.

We return to that Passover meal, when Jesus introduces the first Communion. In the wake of that meal, Jesus warns his disciples of what is going to go down.

In Matthew 26 Jesus makes a very peculiar statement. Verse 31 has him saying, "All of you will be offended at me during this night, for it has been written, 'Strike the shepherd and the sheep will be scattered.'"[4]

Of course, the shepherd is Jesus and the sheep are his disciples. The context of a shepherd being struck down and the sheep being scattered is the work of shepherding. The work of shepherding is the work of protecting

---

4. From the *Orthodox Jewish Bible*. Other English translations insert "I will" to the quote from Zechariah 13:7, which shows the Lord of Hosts speaking. These translations read "I will strike down . . ." The "I will" is not explicit in the Greek or Hebrew.

sheep. The implication is that the shepherd by doing his work is sacrificed and saves his sheep. "No greater a love than this" that a shepherd lay down his life for his sheep. *The context of Jesus being struck down and his disciples scattering is Jesus protecting his disciples with his life.*

The parallel text in John 13, which likewise takes place after the Passover meal, has Jesus speaking specifically to Peter. In verse 36, Peter asks Jesus a question which doesn't appear in Matthew, Mark, or Luke: "Simon Peter said to Him, 'Lord, where are You going?' Jesus answered, 'Where I go, you cannot follow Me now; but you will follow later.'"

Again, Jesus wants his disciples to remain to spread the Word. The only way this can happen is if violent resistance is taken off the table. This is especially important because violent resistance via a battle seemed a desirable choice compared to Roman execution. Going out in a blaze of glory beats the horror of Roman execution. Jesus says, "No! I need you here to go into all the nations and spread the good news. I will be the one and only to bear the horror of Roman execution."

Washing Feet Liberation

I want to for the next few pages turn to the Gospel of John. John is the latest written gospel, composed in the early 100s AD. This means it is written by the disciples of Jesus' first disciples.

John presents the highest Christology of the four Gospels, pointing to Jesus as divine and even uncreated. At the same time, John paints an intimate picture of a master-teacher living, guiding, and ministering alongside his disciples. In many ways, John presents a master-teacher who is divine, who is the face of God to his closest disciples, whom Jesus in turn refers to as friends. For Buddhists, this notion of the teacher as the face of God is easily understood. In the Zen and Tibetan traditions, the teacher is seen as the face of the Buddha and as a conduit of the Buddha's teaching. To Jesus' friends/disciples, Jesus is the equivalent—the face and conduit of God, defined as Father by Jesus himself.

We see the intimate relationship between master-teacher and disciples no clearer than in the foot-washing event. It comes in John 13 at the Passover meal. Matthew, Mark and Luke have the first Communion event. John has the foot-washing event. The foot-washing event is John's Communion. And like the first Communion, the foot-washing event was an intimate moment shared between master-teacher Jesus and his closest disciple-friends.

The foot-washing event purposely foreshadows the cross as well as teaches the way of servanthood. Jesus first points out the conventional truth of servanthood. He wants to teach his disciples the humility needed to be leaders in the building of God's commonwealth. But Jesus says in verse 7 that "what I am doing you don't understand now." If the teaching of humility is the only point, what is not to understand then and there? What is unclear about the lesson at this point?

In the foot-washing event Jesus is foreshadowing the cross, where he will lay down his life for his disciple-friends. Jesus is saying, "Just as I am washing your feet in an act of utter humility, I will in just a couple days liberate your path so you can continue building God's commonwealth. I will liberate your path in the greatest act of humility, death on a Roman cross."

The language of a pathway is purposeful. Clean feet mean pathway-walkers could continue their walking with the *feeling* of being clean and free. Being clean does provide us with a sense of contentment and freedom, doesn't it? There is something significant about feeling clean. This is especially true if the whole body is clean, which Jesus implies is the case in verse 10. So, Jesus cleans his disciples' feet so they can keep on walking, keep on moving, keep on spreading the good news of the Father's love, keep on building God's commonwealth.

But there is real fear even with clean feet and clear hearts. They fear being arrested for following their righteous and revolutionary teacher and facing the same fate he will suffer. Their fear stands in the way of the deep sense of liberation needed to continue in the building of God's commonwealth. Their fear is justified but paralyzing.

Jesus, who profoundly loves his disciples, sees that fear in his friends' eyes and spirits. Their fear profoundly weighs on him. So, Jesus will bear the cross to take away the fear, a justified fear, freeing his disciples in spirit, enabling them to continue in the way of building God's commonwealth.

Jesus washes his disciples' feet so they can physically continue on the way of building God's commonwealth. Parallel to this, Jesus dies on behalf of his disciples and the movement so they can emotionally and spiritually continue in the way of building God's commonwealth.

Jesus himself teaches that his death will initiate the arrival of the Spirit of Truth. Jesus talks about this rather explicitly a little after the foot-washing event, in John 14. Jesus talks about leaving with his disciples the Spirit of Truth, which will teach them everything they need to know when they are without him, recalling in them Jesus' teaching and presence. Jesus says, "Because of my enduring presence through the Spirit of Truth, there is no reason for troubled or fearful hearts." Jesus basically says, "My death will mean liberation from your fear and from the fearful wrath of Rome."

Life Laid Down for Friends

John 15:13 says, "Greater love has no one than this, that one lay down his life for his friends." The only way to fully understand this verse is to again discuss the context confronting Jesus. Again, Jesus faces a choice. What can he do? He sees the utter necessity of God's commonwealth being realized yet faces the worldly power of Rome, an unconquerable power in the eyes of the world.

Collective, violent resistance is an option even if it would contradict all that Jesus has been teaching. It is an option that Barabbas has just recently used. Barabbas is a violent insurrectionist who along with Jesus is arrested for his resistance to Rome's power. However, Barabbas approves of violent resistance.

We read about a choice between Barabbas, a violent insurrectionist, and Jesus, a nonviolent one, in Matthew 27:15–23. The choice between Barabbas and Jesus represents the choice between violent resistance and nonviolent resistance. What do the powers-that-be want to rid themselves of, the violent way of Barabbas or the nonviolent way of Jesus? The powers-that-be choose to rid themselves of the way of nonviolence, knowing that nonviolence is the most lasting and most efficacious way to overcome worldly power and systems.

Jesus sticks with nonviolence. Like Dr. Martin Luther King Jr., Jesus "decides to stick with love." He does so to save his friends, to save them a premature end. His individual death will spare them and allow them to know peace and in turn nonviolently spread the gospel of love, a love that overcomes the gospel of worldly power.

Caiaphas' vs. Jesus' Plan

In the background of Jesus' statement in John 15 that there is no greater love than laying down one's life for a friend is Caiaphas' claim a few chapters before. John 11:47–53 reads:

> So the chief priests and the Pharisees called a meeting of the council, and said, "What are we to do? This man is performing many signs. If we let him go on like this, everyone will believe in him, and the Romans will come and destroy both our holy place and our nation." But one of them, Caiaphas, who was high priest that year, said to them, "You know nothing at all! You do not understand that it is better for you to have one man die for the people than to have the whole nation destroyed." He did not say this on his own, but being high priest that year he prophesied that Jesus was about to die for the nation, and not for the nation only, but to gather into one the dispersed children of God. So from that day on they planned to put him to death. (NRSV)

Caiaphas' great plan was to have Jesus die in order to save the Jewish people in Rome and to somehow reverse the diaspora and unite the Jewish nation in Jerusalem. Jesus' idea was very different. Jesus was going to lay down his life for his friends so that his disciples could continue in his work of preaching radical love. Jesus' job for the disciples, the Great Commission, was to spread the good news. This good news would, organically, from the ground up and from his disciples out, save the nation and all nations from destruction. But this process begins with Jesus freeing the path and the minds of his disciples, leaving them to scatter, regroup, and begin again.

Jesus himself hints at this in John 16:32: "Behold, an hour is coming, and has already come, for you to be scattered, each to his own home, and to leave Me alone" (NASB).

In John 17 Jesus gives his rationale for all of this. Jesus is in Gethsemane contemplating his death to come and praying for his disciples. In Jesus' beautiful prayer, we see his sincere and poignant love for his disciples. In the prayer, he is a proud teacher, a worried best friend, and a protective big brother. And he offers achingly beautiful words:

> "Father, the hour has come; glorify your Son, so that the Son might glorify you, just as you gave him power over all flesh, so that you have given everything to him, that he might give them life in the Age . . . I make supplication on their behalf; I do not make supplication on behalf of the cosmos, but rather on behalf of those you have given to me, because they are yours. And all that is mine is yours, and what is yours is mine, and I have been glorified in them. And I am no longer in the cosmos, and they are in the cosmos, and I am coming to you. Holy Father, keep them in your name, which you have given me, that they may be one just as we are. When I was with them, I protected them in your name, which you gave

> me, and guarded them, and not one of them perished except the son of perdition, so that the scripture might be fulfilled. But now I am coming to you, and in the cosmos I speak these things so that they might have the joy that is mine made full within them. I have given them your word, and the cosmos hated them, because they are not of the cosmos, just as I am not of the cosmos. I pray not that you should take them out of the cosmos, but that you should keep them away from the wicked one. They are not of the cosmos, just as I am not of the cosmos. Make them holy in the truth; the word that is yours is truth. Just as you sent me forth into the cosmos, I sent them also forth into the cosmos."

It seems clear to me that the work Jesus has to finish is dying on behalf of his disciples, "laying down his life for his friends." He will give himself up, "supplicate" himself, to protect the safety and lives of his disciples. While he is still with them, and to the very end, he will protect them. Through his death and his urging them to peacefully let him go, he continues to protect them. Plainly put, because of his supplication, the disciples are not arrested and themselves executed.

In the wake of Jesus' crucifixion, the disciples see Jesus' utter love for them in his becoming their scapegoat. Their seeing of Jesus' utter self-emptying compassion on the cross gives way to them realizing the depth of God's love and the power of imitating Christ's self-emptying compassion.

Profoundly changed by their teacher's love for them and his giving himself up for them, the disciples in turn spread the message of divine love perfectly embodied in their master. "Through their word," people come to trust the truth of Jesus. More disciples give way to more disciples. From this, a lineage of Jesus-followers continues onward and onward. We call this sacred lineage beginning with Jesus the church.

Jesus' Own Cup to Drink

Something else points to Jesus' in-real-time sacrifice on behalf of his disciples. It comes during Jesus' arrest scene. In particular, it comes in the words Jesus uses when forbidding Peter to strike back. Judas leads the Roman authorities to Jesus outside of Gethsemane. He betrays Jesus with a kiss. And the following occurs in the John 18 version of the story:

> Jesus again asked them, "Whom do you seek?" And they said, "Jesus the Nazarene." Jesus answered, "I told you that I am He; so if

you seek Me, let these go their way," to fulfill the word which He spoke, "Of those whom You have given Me I lost not one." Simon Peter then, having a sword, drew it and struck the high priest's slave, and cut off his right ear; and the slave's name was Malchus. So Jesus said to Peter, "Put the sword into the sheath; the cup which the Father has given Me, shall I not drink it?"

We again see in stark terms here the two choices Jesus is faced with: (1) collective violent resistance as desired and attempted by Peter, which would mean glory in battle and a quick end; or (2) individual nonviolent resistance in the form of Jesus demanding no swords and his giving his individual self up for the sake of his movement. Jesus makes clear that "the Father has given me this cup to drink."

Moreover, Jesus highlights his John 17 promise not to lose even one of his disciples. We see how essential this is to Jesus. It is so essential that he dies to make it an actuality. As we know, eventually his disciples will face martyrdom themselves, but it will be when they are spiritually ready to proverbially wash the feet of others.

The Necessary Denials

Peter's three denials follow right after John 17 and after Jesus is taken into custody. Why is Peter, Jesus' closest disciple and the "rock which the church will be built upon," so insistent in denying the truth, especially considering that Jesus predicted it would happen? After all, he had forewarning.

Fear moves Peter's denials. Peter is living these events in real time. He feels the danger and he experiences immense fear.

Peter is terrified of being arrested himself and facing death. Remember, he just de-eared a soldier. Peter is afraid of being found out and facing the same fate as his teacher.

Peter's fear points to the impetus for Jesus to "take the bullet." To take away Peter's fear, which is indicative of all the disciples' fear, Jesus faces their fear and his own fear and gives himself up to face the dire consequences.

There's something else we should consider. Maybe Peter's denials are part of the plan. Denying Jesus and surviving the onslaught would enhance Jesus' plan to have his disciples survive and make the gospel thrive. In this possible scenario, Jesus telling Peter he will deny him three times was not a prediction but a command, one Peter did not like. It turned out to be a self-fulfilling prophecy.

They've All Scattered

Jesus dies without all but one of his disciples around. This fact gives more credence to the idea that Jesus died specifically to save his disciples. John 19 describes who's there.

> ... standing by the cross of Jesus were His mother, and His mother's sister, Mary the wife of Clopas, and Mary Magdalene. When Jesus then saw His mother, and the disciple whom He loved standing nearby, He said to His mother, "Woman, behold, your son!" Then He said to the disciple, "Behold, your mother!" From that hour the disciple took her into his own household.

None of the twelve disciples are explicitly said to be there.[5] They've all scattered. Why? Because the disciples are afraid of being arrested. Peter's denials and the disciples' fleeing the scene are moved by fear.

And for Jesus, it is part of the plan that his disciples should scatter. While it is not mentioned explicitly in scripture, I presume that Jesus commanded that his disciples scatter. Why? Jesus wanted to protect them and the gospel he gave to them. He used their fear to convince them to stay away. It was *his cross* to bear.

Representative Sacrifice

Jesus dies as a representative, *the* representative, of the whole movement he led. Jesus is no cult leader who pridefully believes that the movement is nothing without him and hence will die without him. He knows it is more than just about him. It is about the Father and the commonwealth.

He nonviolently takes his disciples' place on the cross instead of resorting to violence. Because of this, his teaching and his life was able to be propagated and preached—*transmitted*—through his disciples who survive.

In turn, the Pentecost can happen. The church is born because of Jesus taking the disciples' place on the cross. This sacred lineage enabled by Jesus dying for his disciples brings us all the way here.

---

5. Traditionally, the "disciple whom Jesus loved" was presumed to be the author of the Gospel of John, the apostle John himself. However, since scholars increasingly believe the apostle John did not write the gospel, which was written decades after John's death, most scholars don't believe the mystery disciple is John.

Final Thoughts About the Finale

Let's sum up what I am calling "transmitted-substitutiary salvation":

1. Jesus' teaching of the truth of love and his follower's trust in him transformed the disciples prior to Jesus' death and resurrection.
2. Jesus died to literally save his disciples, whom he loved and called "friends," from the fate of dying at the hands of the Roman authorities.
3. The clearest picture of Jesus' uniqueness—his sacrificial death on behalf of his disciples—naturally becomes the focus of the Jesus movement. It eventually becomes reified and universalized.
4. Because Jesus' disciples were saved, they are able to transmit to others the good news of Christ, his teaching, and his life and death *as a teaching that transforms*.
5. Those receiving and internalizing this good news themselves transmitted the good news to a second generation of disciples, and that generation to the subsequent generation, all the way up to the present.
6. The sacred lineage called "the church" is born and spreads throughout the world.
7. Because of the sacred lineage, Christians in turn can say we are inheritors of Jesus' salvation transmitted to us via the lineage of the church, a lineage that was only possible because of Jesus' death to save his disciples from Roman ruin.
8. The self-emptying compassion embodied in Jesus on the cross and commanded to be embodied by his church saves us.
9. This salvation will eventually be realized by all.

Compassion's Salvation

Self-emptying compassion define the salvation that comes to us through Christ's original sacrifice on the cross on behalf of his disciples. This kind of self-emptying compassion doesn't dissipate from generation to generation as the story is told. Such love doesn't lose its power because the one who personified that love died, was resurrected, and ascended two thousand years ago. In fact, it comes alive in us, his followers. The self-emptying compassion embodied in Christ may be beaten down, persecuted, and put into a tomb, but it cannot remain buried, at least as long as someone standing in the lineage of Jesus is telling the story and striving to likewise embody humility and compassion.

— 11 —

The Pluralist Paradigm of the Cross

Jesus as Bodhisattva

THERE is a centuries-old legend that between the ages of twelve and thirty Jesus traveled to India and learned about Buddhism. These lost years were spent studying and practicing the Buddhist dharma. Jesus internalized the dharma on the basis of his own cultural-religious background. He returned to Judea and taught a kind of Buddhist Judaism.

There is no historical evidence for this. Yet there are groups of Indians and Tibetans who hold to it. That the story continues to be sincerely believed around the world itself says a lot. Many of us would like to believe it! And it is an interesting idea to consider.

One thing is for sure, what Christ taught was often very buddhistic. Jesus' teaching, whether knowingly or not, tapped into buddhistic notions such as his teachings on righteous self-emptying, righteous effort amid suffering, the exaltation of the poor and the vulnerable, and the focus on the imminence of truth and the practice of compassion. Marcus Borg's wonderful book *Jesus and Buddha: Parallel Sayings* gives scriptural examples of the interconnections between the two religious founders' teachings. He presents some profound and undeniable affinities between the 2,500-year-old Buddha and the 2,000-year-old Christ.

More than just Jesus' teaching, which is highly underestimated and overlooked in especially conservative Christian circles, his life exemplifies the practice of compassion. Righteous speech, actions, livelihood, and effort, the Eightfold Path's "compassion practices," are all embodied in Jesus' life.

Jesus, According to Buddhists

The Dalai Lama in his book *The Good Heart* calls Jesus a bodhisattva. Thich Nhat Hanh states Jesus is part of his spiritual ancestry and that Jesus and Buddha are brothers. Buddhadasa points to Jesus as an enlightened teacher whose Sermon on the Mount is enough to enlighten if comprehended deeply. Masao Abe points to Jesus as the exemplar of dynamic Shunyata. So Jesus has some Buddhist "street cred," at least to some of the most important Buddhist teachers to the West.

The Dalai Lama's description of Jesus as a bodhisattva is especially powerful and significant. It should be noted, many other Buddhists see Jesus as a bodhisattva. The reason this is so is that the bodhisattva concept contains notions of sacrifice for the salvation of others and even stories of rising up from the realm of death. A bodhisattva is one who is essentially equal in nature to a Buddha, but considers Nirvana as something not to be grasped onto, especially when others suffer. She, the bodhisattva, hears the cries of the world and sees the suffering and cannot turn away. So she lets go of Nirvana to re-enter the world in order to bring others with her to the light of Nirvana. The parallels to Jesus are unmistakable.

Comparing Jesus as bodhisattva to a more modern version of a historical bodhisattva might be helpful.

Bodhisattva Against the Machine

Professor of Religion Diana Pasulka tells a remarkable story involving a class she regularly teaches titled "Buddhism in Popular Culture." Following a lecture in this class, she encountered a student who revealed a tattoo of Thich Quang Duc, the Vietnamese Buddhist monk who in 1963 famously immolated himself as a protest against the state of things in Vietnam and was famously photographed engulfed in flames. The student got his inspiration for the tattoo from a well-known CD cover. The band Rage Against the Machine used the provocative image for their eponymous 1992 record. Knowing the student was a self-proclaimed Christian, Pasulka was surprised by the tattoo. She asked the student how he came to have the monk on his back and where he learned of the story. Pasulka describes his interesting reply and her own internal response:

> He didn't know who the monk was, just that he had seen him on the cover of the Rage Against the Machine CD, thought it was

an image that cohered with the meaning of the crucified Christ, which was the other visible image on his arm. I was too surprised to ask if the student thought that Thich Quang Duc was resurrected in the same manner as Christ . . . In time, I have come to believe that this is precisely what motivated the student to tattoo the monk's image in the first place. He must understand Thich Quang Duc as virtually resurrected due to his violent death for a noble cause, and most important, through his ongoing incarnations in culture. Although the student never stated this directly, his actions, especially his correlation of the monk with the image of the resurrected Jesus, suggests it.[1]

Thich Quang Duc is considered and revered by Vietnamese Buddhists as a bodhisattva. You see images of him at temples throughout Vietnam. Offerings are given to him regularly.

With Thich Quang Duc's veneration as a bodhisattva in mind, the paralleling of Jesus and Quang Duc is even more telling. Jesus had similar political motivations when he willingly asserted himself in a way he knew would get him killed. When Jesus entered Jerusalem on Palm Sunday, he did so for the distinct purpose of cleansing his society of greed and the power-lust behind it. He knew this would cause a stir.

His provocative act led to his crucifixion, which he did not resist, nor did he call for his many followers to stop. In fact, his death on the cross was an act of civil disobedience to point to the injustice and collective harm of Roman occupation and religious appeasement. Tibetans monk in China who have similarly self-immolated themselves in protest are another, more recent parallel to Jesus in ancient Palestine. Definitely, bodhisattvic actions.

Saving Ones

The most popular example of a bodhisattva is Kuan Yin. In China, Taiwan, and in some parts of Japan and South Korea, devotion to Kuan Yin is unparalleled. Stories of Kuan Yin abound. The most prominent of these stories in China and Taiwan involve the legend of Miao Shan, who is believed to be a historic figure but whose tales are *based* on a true story." Included in the tales of Miao Shan's life are narratives of how she, though perfectly blameless and virtuous, is wrongly killed and how in death she takes on the karmic guilt of others. She even goes into the hell realm to bring beings

---

1. Pasulka, "Virtual Religion," 329

back to earth and then into heaven upon her resurrection. Sounds familiar, doesn't it?

There is profound resonance experienced in stories of such selfless sacrifice. We feel a real sense of humanity, humility, and compassion when we hear of someone selflessly giving themselves up to protect another. Holidays throughout the world, such as our Memorial Day, honor veterans who have fallen. On days like 9/11, we remember firefighters and first responders who gave their all, including their lives, in the work of protecting others. These memorials are extra poignant and powerful because we feel such selflessness deep in our bones. We feel it to such an extent that gratitude naturally exudes from us.

That the Christian story has divine selflessness as its central theme explains why Christianity continues to grow in the world. Jesus, God in the flesh, lays down his self and his life for friends and forgives enemies in the process—this offers universal relevance and allure.

There is even more to the story. Jesus' sacrifice and the world's response to it offers even deeper significance. For we can see Jesus' sacrifice as embodying all examples of compassion throughout time. We look at this next.

The Universal Cross?

As someone who holds to the doctrine of universal restoration, I believe, deep in my heart, that all in the end will be reconciled and restored to God, who is Love personified. Salvation will be universal, applying to all.

Christians holding to universalist restoration believe Christ is absolutely pivotal. Christ is actually *the* pivot that makes the end of hell a future reality.

However, a central question arises. Is it Christ and Christ alone I must go through to get to the "no more suffering" of heaven? Even if I am a Buddhist, a Jew, or a Muslim? Is Christ the only sufficient mediator and bridge to God? Traditional Universalists say yes, Christ is the only means to the restoration of all of creation.

Still, in a pluralistic and diverse society, what do we do with the significant example of exclusivism that says only Christ reconciles the Christian and non-Christian alike? How do I on one hand say "only Christ" yet on the other hand completely affirm non-Christians and their faith traditions?

I actually ask myself this question a lot. As a pluralistic Christ-follower, I indeed want to honor my non-Christian brothers and sisters. Is it possible to be a pluralist yet still see Christ as pivotal? Being a pluralist and seeing Christ as pivotal *seems* mutually exclusive. I believe they are not. But how?

In the Beginning, Love . . .

I begin with the beginning. In the beginning, Love was. God as Love is defined by two overarching realities: a universe-wide humility and a universe-wide compassion. These two realities are united in a creative reality many people, myself included, call God.

God as Love unfolded in a flourish of creativity, and the universe expanded and evolved into what it is now. And the universe continues to expand and evolve.

For you Trinitarians out there, in the creative beginning, the self-enclosed yet infinite love of the Trinity—an infinite love undergirding the primordial family of Father God, Mother Spirit, and Offspring Logos—flowed over and was cast into the long arc of time.

The Turn at Compassion

At the pinnacle, the peak, the climax of that arc was an ultimate act of compassion, the event of Christ on the cross.

On the cross, Jesus, the man of constant sorrow, gives away self, sparing his disciples-deemed-friends the same fate, sparing their blood shed with his own blood shed. A nonviolent Jesus accepts and endures a violent death alone as a criminal to save lives, namely his friends and followers. In the process, he forgives. In Christ on the cross, we see the ultimate exemplification of divine self-emptying compassion.

Through this particular event—the event of the cross where Jesus saves his disciples from death and forgives his enemies of their injustice—comes a universal application and reach.

The particular event of the cross led to the resurrection's victory over grief and the Pentecost's birth of the church. The particular event of the cross eventually led to the nonviolent overthrow of the Roman Empire some three hundred years later. In turn, time was divided into a before and after.

Time becomes measured by BC, "Before Christ," and AD, "*Anno Domini*" (which we might translate as the victory of compassion). Time itself is split and eventually this split in time is applied universally, worldwide.

While Common Era (CE) and Before Common Era (BCE) have replaced AD and BC, the figure of Jesus still represents the dividing line.

For me, it is Christ's act on the cross that matters most. His act, his selfless and compassionate act born out of love for his disciples and a commitment to nonviolence, reveals and represents perfect compassion. It is this compassion that measures time, that is the benchmark of time.

The Pivot of the Cross

That benchmark of Christ serves also as a pivot. Compassion, as perfected on the cross, is the pinnacle and pivot point where creation begins its movement back to its source, to God. That pivot point is what God's unfolding of creation led to and it is what commences creation's folding back to God, in creation's return and restoration to God.

We can use the renowned, universal parable of the prodigal son to help us understand this idea. In the story, there is a loving father, who represents God. And there is a son, the prodigal son, who takes his father's gifts and runs away and wastes those gifts. The prodigal pictures for us here the world as a whole. The world took its many gifts and left its divinity, its connection to God.

But there was a pivot point in time, a pivot point where humanity, moved by complete humility and compassion, realized the error of "his" ways. The prodigal world turned back toward God and began the return to God.

That pivot, that turning point, is Christ on the cross, the moment when complete selflessness and compassion is perfectly pictured and made real.

Christ as Universal Compassion

A key question is, can we separate the compassion embodied on the cross from Christ? In one sense, the answer is no, we cannot separate compassion from its embodiment. Without embodiment, compassion is meaningless. Embodiment of compassion is necessary for compassion to be experienced all ways around, from the receiver of compassion to the giver of compassion.

The seminal question then remains. Does Christ *alone* embody compassion?

Certainly, there are many if not countless examples of selflessness and compassion lived out. There are examples in our various religions—from

Muhammad or the Buddha's gracious and selfless teaching of mercy and compassion to examples of saints sacrificing themselves for the benefit of others.

There are examples in everyday life too: neighbors showing humility and kindness toward their neighbors, parents embodying godly love by selflessly loving and caring for their children and others' children.

A modern example of embodied selflessness and compassion especially resonates. The firefighters on September 11, 2001 climbed up staircase after staircase, scaling the Twin Towers. They had no idea what was going on. They surely must have sensed the danger and risk. But they kept ascending anyway.

These many examples of embodied self-emptying compassion, before and after Christ, all tap into that same perfect love that Christ embodied on the cross. In fact, I believe all examples of selflessness and compassion before and after Christ are themselves pictured in, included in, enfolded into that pivotal event of Christ on the cross.

Christ on the cross is a microcosm of all instances of self-emptying compassion in time.

Forward- and Backward-Looking Faith

When I was a boy growing up in church, a big question I had was, "What about those who lived before Jesus who were not mentioned in the Old Testament? How were they saved when Christ on the cross hadn't happened yet?" The answer I got was that those *before* Jesus faithfully looked ahead to the day Jesus would come; those *after* Jesus faithfully looked (and look) back.

Applying this intriguing idea, before Christ, examples of self-emptying compassion throughout the world faithfully looked ahead to the compassion of Christ on the cross. After Christ, examples of self-emptying compassion throughout the world faithfully look back to the compassion of Christ on the cross. We might use the image of a mirror. Examples of self-emptying compassion before Christ and after Christ faithfully mirror Christ's self-emptying compassion. How could they not? Self-emptying compassion is innate to and in Christ. Examples of self-emptying compassion tap into what is innate in Christ.

I go one step further. Examples of self-emptying compassion across time are embedded in the compassion of Christ on the cross. Again, the cross is a microcosm of all real examples of self-emptying compassion throughout time.

He Became Compassion

In church as a kid I learned that the sins of humankind were placed on Christ's shoulders on the cross as he paid the penalty of sin. The idea is that Jesus became sin for us. I don't think this gets at the full magnitude of the cross. With Jesus as all sin, we don't get the complete picture, nor the true power of Christ's compassion.

I believe Christ became compassion on the cross. And all acts of sincere self-emptying compassion throughout time are embodied in Christ's self-emptying compassion on the cross. In Christ's heart we have the heart of humility and compassion, the same heart that moved the countless examples of love in history. In Christ on the cross we have represented all examples of altruistic love throughout time and space. Christ on the cross relinquishes sin with compassion.

There is an archetype in literature and film known as the Everyman. The Everyman represents the ordinary man or woman confronting an extraordinary situation that he wants but cannot avoid. We have a lot of examples of this. Gary Cooper in the film *High Noon* is a perfect example. Cooper is the sheriff, volunteered for the job by some of the town's citizens. He accepts it thinking it's such a peaceful town and a quiet time. When crime and criminals come into the town one day, everything changes. He is forced to face it all alone, despite his fear and vulnerability and lack of experience with things like outlaws. He rises to the occasion as an Everyman.

Jesus on the cross is a real, live Everyman. And in Jesus on the cross, we purely see, in a tragic and magnified way, every act of self-emptying compassion.

On the cross, the sin of fallen humanity was conquered by the compassion of God's image in humanity. Sin died on the cross with "It is finished." Compassion lived on.

And the good news is that this self-emptying compassion seen in the microcosm of Christ on the cross, this self-emptying compassion saves us. Christ's compassion on the cross, and the compassion reflected and refracted in the countless of examples of love and compassion all around us and in time, saves us. Self-emptying compassion—Love—saves us! And in the end Love will save us all.

As for me personally, I can say Jesus saved me in that his life of teaching and his life as a teaching saved me from hopelessness and meaninglessness. I can also say that the cross saved me because without the cross there would be no Gospels and no church through which I received the good news of Christ's teaching and life of love. Jesus saved the disciples firsthand, and because the disciples were in turn able to share the good news through Word and tradition, I received it some 2,000 years later.

— 12 —

Good Friday Blues, Easter Gospel

I RECALL an especially memorable listen of an Elvis Presley record, his Sun Sessions recordings to be exact. My son was five years old and he came up to me while I was listening and took to liking it. Excited about this, I gave an ad hoc history lesson on Elvis in a way a five-year-old could understand. I showed him pictures of Elvis on the Web and even showed the young Elvis performing "Jailhouse Rock."

Amid all of this, he asked me a question that he used to ask whenever talking about someone from the past. It is a question that arose after his grandfather died when he was just four. "Is he in heaven?" It was Corey's way of asking if someone was dead.

At first, I chuckled a bit, thinking about the cultural joke that Elvis is still alive and living on earth somewhere. Then I got serious. I answered truthfully.

"Yes, Elvis is in heaven." Corey became upset at this, having taken a liking to Elvis rather quickly. "No, he is not in heaven! No, he is still here, right Daddy?!"

I tried to assuage him with the notion that because his music is still with us, he is still with us, and thus he lives-on in a way. Of course, being a five-year-old, Corey had some difficulty with the abstractness of this. But I think he got the essence of what I was saying. At least, he stopped crying and went on to the next thing.

Yet, thinking about our sweet conversation afterward, I realized how we humans have an innate need for Easter. We all want to see those we love again. We want something to continue after the loss of a loved one. Most cannot fathom that this life is the end. We desire a resurrection so that reunions with those we've lost and deeply miss are possible. We want to see loved ones in heaven again. We want to see Elvis again.

There is an emotional need behind the story of Jesus coming back after his disciples and friends thought he was gone.

Easter is a sacred metaphor of experiencing, when we need it most, a way arising out of the no-way of grief.

The Original Easter

The Easter story, the original Easter story, points to the basic paradigm of loving, losing, grieving, and somehow finding wholeness despite the despair.

As we've discussed, the relationship between Jesus and his disciples was more than just a teacher-student relationship. Jesus expressed love for them and called them his "friends." They were blood brothers walking the dusty trails of ancient Palestine together, eating together, learning together, serving the community together. The bond was real and profound.

As for the disciples, they often called him "Lord." In modern lingo, we might translate "Lord" as "my greatest friend and beloved mentor."

Imagine fearfully fleeing your greatest friend and beloved mentor at his darkest moment. This is what the disciples had to do. It would be the equivalent of a soldier leaving his commander and comrade alone in the heat of the battle, leaving him to die.

The disciples had to flee. It was necessary that Jesus' disciples scatter so as not to be gathered up, arrested, and possibly executed themselves. Not scattering and being arrested would have meant the gospel would have likely died with the disciples.

Still, the grief the disciples felt in the aftermath was wrenching. That grief was compounded by the unbearable heaviness of guilt, a kind of survivor's guilt. That grief and guilt cannot be underestimated.

If the grief and guilt was not assuaged, who knows what the lives of the disciples would have amounted to. Jesus' return was necessary to comfort and save his friends from the turmoil of their grief and guilt.

This is what we call the resurrection: Jesus' returning to comfort and salve the hearts of those grieving and guilt-laden. And it was indeed transformative, eventually leading to the Pentecost and the development and lineage of the church.

Such experiences of spiritual resurrection, of sensing life despite loss, help us to face the reality of loss. These experiences help us to persevere through the brutal reality that things change, that we lose what we love, that the comfortable normal changes into the painful abnormal.

And as is true with the grieving process, whether it be grief over losing a loved one or in losing our comfortable norm, from the fire of loss eventually comes the growth of a new forest. Yes, scars of that fire remain, but the soil is stronger, more resilient, more enduring.

The fire of loss that is the crucifixion gives way to the seedling of new life in spite of loss—this is the resurrection. And the resurrection in turn gives way to the new forest that is the Pentecost.

Easter Spirituals, Easter Blues

Elvis was at his artistic best when he was singing the Blues and Gospel music. He learned the Blues in the Black clubs and dance halls of Memphis. He learned the spirituals and Gospel in church, both his own church and a Black church, where he would sometimes go to hear Black Gospel.

Elvis discovered in Black music power and joy. He discovered the music's life-giving way amid the life-denying realities all around in his poor neighborhood in Memphis. For African-Americans, it went deeper. They knew and experienced the life-denying realities of slavery, Jim Crow, and racism. Black spirituals and the Blues, for Black people, served as a simile for the Easter story.

One of my favorite books is James Cone's *The Spirituals and the Blues*. In this book, Cone interprets and explicates the connection between Black spiritual music and the Blues, saying spirituals pointed to eternal hope beyond despair while the Blues pointed to the temporal hope found in being honest about despair. Both point to the subversive claim that circumstances around us may say "no way," but our spirits, fueled into music and fueled *by* music, say, "yes way." In spirituals and the Blues there is an unsparing honesty about despair and death. At the same time, there is a defiance in the face of the external reality, a defiance filled with the hope of life, with new life embodied in the resurrection and continued in the Pentecost.

Dr. Cone puts it like this:

> Herein lies the meaning of the resurrection. It means that the cross was not the end of God's drama of salvation. Death does not have the last word. Through Jesus' death, God has conquered death's

power over his people . . . The resurrection is the divine guarantee that black people's lives are in the hands of the Conqueror of death . . . They don't have to cry anymore.[1]

Easter represents the process of escaping the mire of our old lives and realizing the light of new life. And it is especially poignant when contemplating the despair of grief, of losing what we once held close. This is the story of the original Easter, and of every Easter before and since.

Psalms 23 Peace

A spiritual Elvis loved to sing was a new spiritual written by African-American composer Thomas Dorsey for the famed gospel singer Mahalia Jackson. It incorporates themes from the ancient song known as the Twenty-Third Psalm. Dorsey's gospel song is called "Peace in the Valley." It speaks to the Easter message of hope rising out of despair, peace found despite the valley of the shadow of death, and a presence of light and love leading us to a new life of green pastures, still waters, right paths.

I will end by offering a lyric from this new spiritual, and let it serve as an Easter prayer.

> There the flow'rs will be blooming, the grass will be green
> And the skies will be clear and serene
> The sun ever shines, giving one endless beam
> And the clouds there will never be seen
> There the bear will be gentle, the wolf will be tame
> And the lion will lay down by the lamb
> The beasts from the wild will be led by a child
> I'll be changed from the creature I am

---

1. Cone, *Spirituals and the Blues*, 93

— 13 —

The Resurrection and Ascension's Wideness

The Forgotten Day

I GREW up in a very devout Christian household. Yet the ascension is something I don't remember family members or church folks talking much about. I still don't hear much about it. The crucifixion? Good Friday remembers and honors the crucifixion. And the whole Christian faith revolves around what's remembered and honored on that sacred day. The resurrection? The second biggest Christian holiday celebrates the resurrection. We call it Easter. But the ascension?

Sure, the Christian calendar includes a Sunday dedicated to the ascension. The lectionary includes a scripture reading about it. But I for one have never heard a sermon about it.

Always one to lift up an underdog, I want to lift up this underdog of a Christian holy day known as the ascension. First, it might help for me to give a refresher on what I think the two events—the crucifixion and the resurrection—leading up to the ascension mean. This is a kind of summary of my thinking on what the two central events of the Christian tradition mean.

The Crucifixion Reviewed

I've already discussed this in chapter 10, but it is so essential that I discuss it briefly again below.

The traditional view of Christ's death is that Christ died for us. He died in our and all of humanity's place, for our sins and the penalty of our sins, which is death. The fancy theological term for this is "substitutiary atonement." We are deserving of death and suffering because of our sins. But Jesus became humanity's substitute on the cross. And through his being our substitute, we are atoned, we are put right in the eyes of God.

I should say here that traditional Universalists believe all of this. They simply make the claim that Jesus atoned for the sins of *all* on the cross and that all will be reconciled because of the cross, namely Jesus' pivotal, transforming work on the cross.

As for me, I hold to what I have call and describe as the "transmitted-substitutiary" view of the actual crucifixion. Succinctly put, Jesus directly died for his disciples and followers to save them from Roman persecution and execution. They are transformed by this ultimate act of compassion, their teacher's laying down his life for them, his friends. They also live to tell the tale. Consequently, the good news of God's love can be shared with subsequent generations. The sharing of the good news ultimately comes via the Gospels and the New Testament, and through the church. Generation after generation, this gospel has been transmitted. And the transmission of Light continues.

The Resurrection Reviewed

If the crucifixion is the historical reason for a religion holding Christ's name, the resurrection is the emotional, spiritual reason. And the resurrection is real.

What is remarkable about the Easter story is that Jesus' primary focus upon his return is to comfort his disciples in their grief, so they are emotionally and spiritually able to create the church. He does not visit Pontius Pilate to show him the error of his every way. He does not go to the soldiers to say how much more powerful he is than their big weapons, big cross, big examples of violence. He does not go to the religious hierarchy to express how wrong and full of it they are. He does not show up in the temple in Jerusalem on the Sabbath to exhibit that he is the way, truth, and life. No, he goes to his disciples, his friends. He goes to comfort them, to let them know they are forgiven, to encourage them to keep his spirit alive by spreading the way of love he preached, lived and died for.

We see Jesus' ministry to his grieving disciples most clearly in Jesus' interaction with Peter. Now, Peter plays the common man in the Bible. He represents all us ordinary blokes and blokettes. He is our stand-in, really, in the Gospels.

Peter denied his friendship, his followership, his fellowship with Christ three times, as Jesus said he would. Jesus needed those denials to happen, not wanting to implicate his friends. But the pain for Peter wasn't any less. After Peter denied Jesus, in one of the most heartbreaking ends of a narrative, scripture says Peter went out and wept bitterly.

When Jesus died, Peter was dealing with profound grief and profound regret. All the disciples and followers of Jesus were.

Profound grief and profound regret—that is the human life in a nutshell, isn't it? We must deal with the reality of loss and the reality of brokenheartedness. Human beings can't escape it. Buddhism calls this inescapable reality of loss and brokenness the First Truth.

What's more, Christ, the divine one, the picture of God, comes to the bloke-like-us Peter in the depth of his despair in the wake of his teacher's physical death. Jesus returns to Peter and takes Peter's three greatest failures and gives him a second chance, gives redemption.

Jesus asks Peter "Do you love me?" three times. With each answer of yes, Jesus gives a command to Peter: "Feed my sheep." It is a command that amounts to a command to take care of people. Failures are turned into affirmations of love and commands of good work to do.

In other words, Christ's return says to all of us weighed down with grief and regret, "I am here. I am not really gone or lost or dead. Your second chance begins now, in this very moment." In the words of Michael Card, "My child, begin again, you're free to start again."

For Peter, with this weight lifted, he can begin again. In so doing, he becomes what he is meant to be—the Rock, the foundation of the church.

Focus on Ascension

Now we come to the ascension. What is the ascension?

It is Jesus' true physical departure. Even Christ must physically leave this world. We cannot possess the unpossessable. We cannot confine what is eternal.

In these valleys of doubts and darkness, when God is more transcendent than imminent, more external to us than internal, when God must himself depart and we must remain, we are forced to look to the goodness next to us. We are forced to internalize the goodness in creation, in fellow sojourners, in the breaths we are given.

The ascension says something else. It says the most essential thing about Christ's resurrection is not his *physical* presence with us but his *spiritual* presence with us. Christ's body departs, but Christ's spirit never leaves nor forsakes us.

What makes Christ's presence redemptive for his followers is not his physical presence. It is his spiritual presence. It is his spiritual presence that gives us a second chance and helps us to keep going, helps us to keep loving one another as we live our lives.

Remaining Questions

As I close, I'd like to ask a couple questions. Were Jesus' friends and disciples sad those days after Jesus ascended into heaven? I think it is clear they were. They grieved his physical absence as we all would.

There is another big question: were they as sad as they would have been if Jesus did not return? In other words, was the pain after Christ's spiritual ascension as severe as the pain after Christ's physical death? Absolutely not.

Why? Because his disciples had witnessed what we put our faith in: that when it comes to the spirit of things, there is no death. When it comes to the spirit of things, in the words of Thich Nhat Hanh, "there is no birth, there is no death."

The disciples experienced this firsthand. Their eyes were opened to the truth that the Spirit never dies. The Spirit never leaves us nor forsakes us.

It is as if in his return to his disciples and followers Jesus says, "Remember, I won't always be physically with you, I will return to the Father. But lo, I will be with you always, even until the end of the earth."

— 14 —

Pentecost's Plan

THERE are a few metaphors the New Testament uses for the church. The first is given by Jesus himself in the Gospel of John, chapter 15. It comes pre-Pentecost, of course. Yet Jesus makes clear in verse 5, "I am the vine and you [my followers] are the branches." In other words, the church is an extension of Jesus.

The apostle Paul offers another metaphor throughout his epistles. For Paul, the church is the singular body of Christ, with Christ as the head of that one body. Again, the church is the extension of Christ. Jesus is the foundation of the church, the mind and brain of the church, and Jesus's Spirit, his Breath, pervades the church. In turn, the church is Christ's visible representation in and to the world. The church is the heart and hands of Christ working and applying the mind of Christ here and now.

Lastly, there is the metaphor-laden term used for the early church in the book of Acts, "the Way." Reference to the earliest Christian church as "the Way" occurs some five times.[1] Paul, defending himself before a Roman court, specifically claims the name. "I admit that I worship the God of our ancestors as a follower of the Way." The name seems to derive from Jesus calling himself "the Way" in John 14:6, a verse Evangelicals memorize as soon as they are able to speak. Jesus was the Way for his disciples and followers. With his departure via the ascension, and the arrival of his church at Pentecost, the church becomes the Way. Again, the church as the Way is an extension of Jesus as the foundational Way.

---

1. Acts 9:2; 19:9; 19:23; 24:14, 19.

What does this paradigm that the church is an extension of Christ mean? It means a lot!

The Church as Spiritual Parent

There is a saying in the Catholic tradition, "There is no salvation without the church." An Evangelical rendition of this is the notion of a spiritual father or mother. A spiritual father or mother is basically a Christian—and thus, according to Evangelicals, a member of the universal church—who "brought you to the Lord." In non-Evangelicalese, a spiritual parent is someone who shared with you the good news of Christ and who fostered an internalization of Christ, an "accepting of Christ into your heart." Simply put, a spiritual parent is a representative of the church who births someone's conversion to the Christian faith.

This notion of the spiritual parent is interesting. The spiritual parent is someone who has already internalized Christ, who has taken Christ into their heart. They come to another as an extension of Christ. They proselytize as a representative of the church in the work of bringing more to Christ and more into the church. And there is no salvation without a spiritual parent.

Knowledge of Christ being essential to salvation, the church's primary work is to share knowledge of Christ. Jesus himself gave the church its marching orders—"make disciples of our fellow human beings." This entails writing literature, holding Bible studies, doing door-to-door evangelism, Billy Graham "crusades," and/or having church services every Sunday morning. As disciples of Christ gathered as the church, and as the extension of Christ on earth, the call is to make more disciples and extend Christ throughout the earth.

Spreading Compassion

Divine compassion saves and will save all. I believe divine compassion was embodied and made complete in Christ. However, divine compassion saved before Christ and saves where the name of Christ is unknown.

For centuries, Christians have discussed and debated the status of "the unevangelized." The discussion and debate, which continues to this very day, revolves around the question of what happens to those—past, present, and future—who've never heard the name Christ or the good news of

Christ. There is no clear answer. And the Bible, used in the Christian faith to answer our questions, is unclear. But answers are offered.

On one end, there are those who rigidly declare that the unevangelized will face the judgment of God and because of a lack of faith in Christ will face the reality of hell. This holds true whether one has heard the name of Christ or not. Though harsh, the Bible is clear, according to the "strict constructionists," that faith in Christ is the only way to heaven.

Thankfully, on the other, saner end, there are those who posit that a second chance post-death will be offered where the good news of Christ will be revealed, and a decision allowed whether to accept or reject Christ, hence deciding one's fate.

In the same inclusivity vein, others point to Romans 1:20 and contextualize that if a faith in some notion of God and godly providence exists, then salvation will be granted. This is known as the general revelation argument. Those who see God revealed generally in creation and internalize this general revelation will be saved.

I hold to this general revelation approach. However, connecting the general revelation of God in creation to the specific revelation of God in Christ seems necessary. *What connects the general revelation of creation and the specific revelation of Christ is compassion.*

Compassion is found throughout creation, in the human domain and the non-human domain. The compassion that Christ embodied and revealed is mirrored throughout creation. Whenever someone selflessly takes care of another or protects and shelters another or expresses and shows true love toward another, the compassion of Christ is seen. Compassion, whether generally revealed in creation or specifically embodied in Christ, saves us. And compassion will save all via the work of Christ's extension on earth, the church.

The Never-Ending Work

What is the work of the church? To make disciples, and thereby build the commonwealth of God and assure the salvation of all. The ultimate aim is not individual salvation but to remake Eden—another term, the earliest term, for the commonwealth of God. Who belongs in the commonwealth? Those who've internalized the way of compassion and humility. This is the Way that Christ perfected and made complete. This is the Way the church is called to continue in.

Hence, the church preaches Christ and his way of compassion and humility. What's more, in cultures that are not Christian (e.g., Buddhist, Islamic, or Jewish), the church points to the way of compassion and humility living or latent in religious traditions and teachings alive in those other cultures. The church of Christ partners with other religious communities, pointing to the compassion embedded in the religious traditions therein and in turn showing how such compassion parallels Christ's perfect compassion and utter humility, namely on the cross.

In Mark 9, Jesus offers us the missional paradigm of pointing to and highlighting compassion already living or latent in other faiths. In verses 38–40, Jesus' disciples come to him angry at some healers doing their healing work using Christ's name. The disciples tell Jesus to command that they stop. Jesus instead corrects his disciples. He states, "Do not stop him, for no one who does a miracle in my name can in the next moment say anything bad about me, for whoever is not against us is for us."

In other words, the point is the healing, and the building of the commonwealth as a result. If there is healing in the name of Christ, in the name of God, or in the name of Love (which God is), then those doing such compassionate healing both build the commonwealth and are included in the commonwealth.

The missional paradigm of highlighting the compassion-teachings in other faith traditions and connecting them to the compassion of Christ requires a great deal of work. It requires an openness to garner knowledge about other faith traditions. It also requires the actual practice of garnering such knowledge. It further requires the practice of connecting the compassion-teachings in other traditions to the compassion actualized by Christ, showing that they share in the source of All compassion, God who is Love.

Compassion and humility are the key to inclusion in the commonwealth. The wisemen who visit Jesus are not converted to Judaism but to the way of compassion and humility latent in their own religious traditions. Jesus did not convert the centurion to Judaism upon seeing his compassion and humility toward his servant. He pointed to the compassion and humility already there and included the centurion in the commonwealth.

Pastoral Care

We might call this missional paradigm the pastoral care model. To better understand the model, I use myself as an example.

I am a pastor. I have been a pastor some twelve years, including eight years as a hospice chaplain. My ultimate aim as a pastor in a public, interfaith setting is to be what those I am pastoring need me to be. For the Buddhist, I aim to fill in as a Buddhist, relying on my years of studying the beautiful tradition and my often-unconscious application of its approach. For a Jew, I try to touch my Jewish ancestral roots (my great-grandmother was Jewish) and inhabit the Jewish tradition as best I can. For a Baptist, I recall my own Baptist background and apply it to the context at hand. For a Catholic, I remember my Polish grandfather, who sometimes took me to Mass, and I attempt to care for Catholics as I cared for him. For the agnostic, I tap into my many questions about the meaning of it all.

The apostle Paul once provocatively wrote, "I have become all things to all people so that by any possible means I might [liberate some]."[2] Buddhists might call this approach the practice of *upaya*, the practice of meeting and pastoring people where they are.

The work of the church in a world filled with various faiths and spiritual approaches is similar. The church is to become all things to all people in the aim of building the compassionate commonwealth. For me, this means pointing to compassion where it is found and connecting it to the boundless compassion of the Cosmic Christ.

The Endless Work of Universal Reconciliation

God is portrayed as a loving parent who runs to embrace prodigal sons and a good shepherd who seeks every lost sheep. God will not give up till all of creation is reconciled.

Christ via the church will not give up either. Christ and his church's compassion will endlessly do the work of salvation. Neither Christ's work nor the church's work ends with the end of the world as we know it. The missional work of divine compassion is eternal work, and it will surely realize the divine will that none should perish and that all should know eternal life in God.[3]

---

2. 1 Corinthians 9:22.
3. 2 Peter 3:9.

To borrow from the Buddhist tradition, the church is akin to a bodhisattva collective. She, the body of Christ, hears the sounds of suffering and cannot turn away. The bodhi of Christ turns toward the suffering and reaches out endlessly to save. She won't rest in the freedom of heaven until all are included, for there is no rest nor freedom when suffering remains real.

— 15 —

My Confession

I must be honest that sometimes when I am preaching I can hear my mother and father in the back of my head. It usually happens when I say something that I know they'd disagree with. Knowing Evangelical culture and what makes it tick, mom and dad would say that that voice isn't really theirs but the Holy Spirit's. The Holy Spirit is "the keeper of correct doctrine," and "he" is convicting me.

I tend to think that voice in my head is really my innate need to feel my parents' and my family's acceptance. It is a need to be loved, as Mr. Rogers would say, "just the way you are." It is a need to know that you innately belong where you first felt belonging. This longing for belonging does not leave.

However, part of being a mature adult means that you are honest with yourself and that you are your true self with others. Censoring yourself, putting on a front to please even your family, prevents you from being who you are and realizing who you are.

All that said, we should be clear. The vast majority of the world does not see Jesus as savior of the world. Most Christians do. But do I?

My Truth

As with most things, if we are honest with ourselves, most matters of faith are rarely clear-cut, black or white, or as simple as a cliché or creed. Sometimes there are no simple yes or no answers. Is "Is Jesus the savior of the world?" a question like this?

I unpack my answer with these words: the love and compassion of God, which Jesus represented, is at the heart of the world's salvation. Jesus represented the love and compassion of God not with his body, with what Paul calls the flesh. It was not Jesus' physical prowess or his intellectual capacity. In these instances, Jesus was pretty normal.

Thankfully, there are countless examples of weak and withered bodies and intellectually limited human beings exemplifying immense love and compassion. In fact, examples of love and compassion amid impossible situations are the examples that we remember most, that live into the future even after the body dies.

Love and compassion are a heart thing. Love and compassion come from something essential in us. They come from something connected to God and thus eternal. They endure forever—even if in memory and in the stories we continually tell—though the body does not.

Preceding the Blood

Even if we submit that Jesus on the cross means the salvation of the world, we must ask, what about Jesus on the cross saved? Some say his body and blood, pointing to the idea of Jesus being the sacrificial lamb for human beings and their sin. They point to scripture to support this.

However, I cannot agree. Why? Because something preceded Jesus offering his body and blood to save others. What preceded Jesus' sacrifice was Jesus' intention, his will, his heart, which did not take the route of self-preservation but gave self away.

Jesus' godly love and compassion came before his body and blood were given. Without the utter love and compassion in Jesus' heart, there would have been no giving of body and blood. Would the story, the significance of Christ's passion be the same if he resisted, fought, and hated his enemy in the process? What if Jesus never said those words "thy will be done" but said "I can't," and escaped, fought, and hated until he could flee and fight no longer? Yes, his fate would inevitably have been the same. Rome would have found him, and he would have died. But without the compassion-moved moment of self-emptying in Gethsemane, the cross would have been completely different.

Essential to the traditional teaching on Jesus' salvation-giving death is that Jesus gave himself up, that he submitted to God's love-induced plan to save the world and forgave his enemies in the process. If Jesus did not empty self in Gethsemane, if Jesus rejected his role, if Jesus disobeyed God's plan, there would have been a huge hole in the plan.

If Jesus followed his natural human desire to escape and flee, though he'd eventually be found, arrested, and crucified, Jesus would not have been blameless, his body and blood would not have remained pure. But his blamelessness and pureness of spirit are essential to the traditional story of Jesus' salvation-giving death.

Concisely put, Jesus' declaration of "thy will [of love] be done" is absolutely fundamental to everything that follows.

Christ: The Essentials

So, as I have noted, it is Jesus' selfless love and compassion that are most essential here. They preceded his giving of himself. His love and compassion enabled him to accept arrest and in so doing to take the place of his disciples and followers, who would have surely died along with him if he had not accepted his fate.

It was a prime example of mind over matter, heart over body.

What's more, and this explains my focus of Jesus as transformational teacher, Jesus' love and compassion is directly connected to his role as rabbi, as teacher.

Jesus as a teacher gave his life on a Roman cross. He did so to teach the world, yes, but also to save his disciples from being arrested and crucified alongside him. He gave himself up so that his disciples could be free.

He was willing to take their place at all costs. That is what makes Jesus a transformational teacher—his complete selflessness on behalf of his disciples.

It is love and compassion, a love and compassion evident most profoundly in Jesus, that essentially saves. The body and blood shed is just a product of the love and compassion that submitted and said, "I am willing to die to save my disciples."

Thy will be done. The will of love and compassion, embodied in God as loving Father, be done.

The One and Only?

But does the will of love and compassion perfected in Jesus *alone* save the world? Is Jesus Christ the only true savior even if you are a Buddhist or a Jew, for example?

Well, we must answer this question first. Are there other examples of the kind of love and compassion Jesus exemplified on the cross? Is the godly will of love and compassion found in more than just Jesus Christ?

Yes, absolutely. Other figures throughout time have embodied love and compassion at a profound and transformational level. For example, the Buddha giving away an easy and comfortable life for sixty years of poverty, constant traveling, and homelessness, all for the purpose of teaching the truth of wisdom and love, comes to mind. There are saints in many traditions that exemplify great and life-saving compassion.

The love and compassion they lived out is the same love and compassion of God that Jesus perfected in his life. It is this sacred love and compassion that saves us.

So, yes, the love and compassion of God found in Christ, lived out by Christ, embodied by Christ, saves the world. But the love and compassion of God, though fully embodied in Jesus, is not found *only* in Jesus. It is found in transformational and selfless teachers throughout time. It is found in heroic and selfless acts of people attempting to protect and serve others. And these examples of compassion participate in Christ's compassion.

We see acts of selflessness and compassion often. During very dark and trying times, people rise to the occasion and give of themselves in heroic ways. When killers in Dallas and Baton Rouge in 2016 cowardly ambushed police officers, there were others, police and regular citizens, who responded by going toward the gunshots out of their compassion-moved duty to protect and serve. We hear stories across cultures about mothers and fathers facing natural disasters or accidents doing everything and giving everything to save their children. For example, a mother amid the shooting in Dallas fell on her four children to protect and save their lives, and was shot. When the officers that were shot were rushed to the hospital, an African-American surgeon in Dallas and a White American in Baton Rouge both tried to save, protect, and serve them. And when they couldn't, when those eight officers died, they offered sincere empathy and compassion. When 9/11 happened, firefighters and police officers climbed the Twin Towers to save others. These are examples of the love and compassion of God evidenced in real time. That was the love and compassion of God applied and lived out.

Salvation: The Essentials

The love and compassion of God at work everywhere in creation is what saves us from isolation and disconnection and separateness. It is the love and compassion of God at work in creation that Jesus took and infused in his life to the highest degree. Christ's uniqueness is not that he is somebody that saved the world. His uniqueness comes in the extent to which his heart loved and embodied compassion in this life. Christ's love and compassion meant he could not forsake his disciples, his followers, those trusting that God's love and compassion never failed. It was his love and compassion; it was the essence of love infused in a soul's life and death; it was God as Love in the spirit of this transformational rabbi; it was his loving and nonviolent heart that could not remain in the tomb but rose and lived on as it always does.

The body went away, ascending into heaven. The love, well, that remains. Making the love that remains as actual and applied on earth as it is in heaven, that is the Christian task.

— 16 —

Christ's Bodhi Tree

JESUS once asked, "But you, whom do you say me to be?"

The question still resonates across the ages. It has been resonating and prodding hearts ever since it was first asked in the days of Jesus' sojourn with his disciples. Jesus asked it to the disciple he'd declare the Rock upon which the church would be built.

Peter received the question and spoke his truth. In Mark, we have the most concise answer: "And in reply Peter said to him, 'You are the Anointed.'"

Peter's answer gives us the earliest and simplest version of the Christian confession and creed. Jesus is the Christ. Or Jesus is Lord. Jesus affirmed it as utterly true, and hence sufficient.

Who is Christ for me? And what is the significance of his birth and life, death and resurrection? I want to myself answer these questions and lay out who Jesus is for me and base it in ancient precedence, that of the early, early church.

Precedence Matters

Let me first say something about the *importance* of historic precedence. There is a word that can otherwise be positive but in this case is not so much. That word is "innovative." When it comes to one's career or starting a business or marketing a product, being innovative is a terrific thing. But when it comes to religious faith, being innovative is not always so terrific. Coming up with your own idea regarding ultimate things void of connection to those who've gone on before you—I think this is a questionable venture. For one thing, it too easily dismisses those who've gone before. It amounts to us saying, "Your old ideas and ways are, well, antiquated and irrelevant. We need something new and improved. And here, I've got it for you." It also means contradicting those ancient and truthful words, "there is nothing new under the sun."

As an 80s kid, I think of the New Coke disaster in the mid-80s. This is a good example of how being innovative when tradition and history matter to so many is prone to failure. So, connecting what I believe to what other Christians in the ancient past believed is crucial when I ponder these things.

This I Believe

Here is what I believe about Jesus. First and foremost, Jesus is my master-teacher. He is my primary guide in the spiritual life.

Based on Jesus being my first-and-foremost master-teacher, I believe in Jesus Christ. Christ, I should mention, is not Jesus' last name. Mary and Joseph Christ didn't have a son named Jesus Christ. Christ is a title meaning Messiah or Anointed One. I believe Jesus was anointed. He is my Messiah. Yes, to quote the earliest and simplest Christian creed, Jesus is Lord.

And I believe because Jesus is the Anointed One, he is also the Son of God. Let me explain this.

As Jewish scholar Daniel Boyarin explains, when ancient Jews heard the title Son of God, they connected it to another title, that of king of Israel. In the Hebrew Scriptures, the king of Israel is often stated as a begotten son of God.[1] But during the time of Jesus there was no king. They were waiting for one. Israel was waiting for a heroic, human messiah to come and take the throne. They were waiting for a new David, a messiah-king, also known as the Son of God.

Boyarin states, "When Mark in the very beginning of his Gospel writes, 'The Beginning of the Gospel of Jesus Christ, the Son of God,' the Son of God means the human Messiah, using the old title for the king of the House of David."[2] This is to say, believing Christ is the Messiah in some sense can mean believing he is the Son of God.

---

1. Psalm 2:7–9; 45:7–8; 82:1–8; 9:26–28; 2 Samuel 7:13–16; Isaiah 9:6.
2. Boyarin, *Jewish Gospels*, 26.

That said, in the traditional Christian sense, Jesus as the Son of God means seeing Jesus as divine. And I believe Jesus was divine. Jesus was a pure conduit of God and godly love. Being a pure conduit of God is my definition of divinity.

I don't believe Caesar, the all-powerful head of an empire, was the son of God as the Romans did. I don't believe Romulus, the founder and first king of Rome, ascended into heaven to be seated on the right hand of God as the Romans believed. I believe a Jewish carpenter from the backwaters of Nazareth who taught love and died in the practice of love is the Son of God, an enlightened, divine being who came to bring justice and liberation to the poor and the outcast.

Divine Adoption

That said, let's look at the New Testament's calling Jesus "the Son of God." This happens most notably in the Gospel of Mark. The point of the Gospel of Mark is to show Jesus as the Son of God. It is in Mark that God directly declares Jesus to be "my beloved Son." And the timing of this divine declaration is extremely significant.

There is an ancient belief of the early, early Christian church called "adoptionism." Many of the earliest Christians held to an adoptionist view of Christ's divinity. Scholars believe that the Jewish Christians that followed Christ and began the early church held to this view. Adoptionism holds that Christ was adopted as God's son, namely upon his baptism. Christ becomes divine upon his baptism with the words, "this is my beloved Son."

Mark, our earliest gospel, written some thirty to forty years after Jesus ascended, implies this belief. The Gospel of Mark does not begin with a miraculous Nativity story or anything like it.

If Mark knew and believed the Nativity story, you'd think he would have included it. If Mark knew and believed the Nativity story, you'd think it too important a piece *not* to include. Paul's writings, which were written before Mark, also don't mention a miraculous birth.

Mark begins with Jesus' baptism and the actual moment of adoption. Mark 1: 9–11 says:

> Jesus came from Nazareth of Galilee and was baptized by John in the Jordan. And when he came up out of the water, immediately he saw the heavens being torn open and the Spirit descending on him

like a dove. And a voice came from heaven, "You are my beloved Son; with you I am well pleased."

Scholars believe that later gospels, Matthew and Luke, written some twenty years later, added the Nativity story as we know it.

In Mark, the earliest gospel, Christ's divine status comes into full fruition when, as an enlightened, wise, and compassionate adult, he accepts the call to follow the plan of God, that of love and justice.

The conception of Christ as the Son of God was a spiritual conception, a spiritual conception of the Holy Spirit. The Holy Spirit spiritually conceived Christ's divinity upon his baptism, when like a dove the Holy Spirit descended and came upon Jesus. That was his spiritual birth, his spiritual awakening. Buddhists might call this Christ's *sopadhishesa-nirvana*, his this-life enlightenment. Literally, Nirvana with a remainder.[3]

Forward to the Past

Paul points to a later point of adoption. Paul in Romans 1 describes God declaring Jesus to be the Son of God at the resurrection. In the original Greek it looks like a poem. Here are verses 3-4: "Concerning his Son—born from David's seed according to the flesh, Marked out by resurrection of the dead as God's Son in power according to a spirit of holiness—Jesus the Anointed, our Lord."

Scholars suggest that in this passage Paul quotes from an earlier tradition, earlier than even Mark, that began in the wake of Jesus' ascension. This earlier tradition believed Jesus was adopted as the Son of God upon his *resurrection*. Not his baptism as Mark tells us, but his resurrection some three years after his baptism.

This resurrection view of adoptionism, that Christ became divine at his resurrection, came first. Resurrection adoptionism was the original understanding. Mark, a later tradition, pushed Christ's divine adoption to earlier in his life, to his baptism. Matthew and Luke, pushed Christ's divinity even earlier, to his birth. And John, the latest written gospel, put Christ's divinity in the very beginning of creation.

As the early church progressed, the New Testament texts were written in time, beginning with the Epistle to the Romans (AD 57–58) and then the

---

3. James C.G. Dunn, *Christology in the Making*, 251–258; Bart Ehrman, *How Jesus Became God*, 111ff

Gospels of Mark (AD 65–73), Matthew and Luke (AD 80–90), and ending with the Gospel of John (AD 90–110). As these texts were written in time, the timing of Jesus as divine morphs. Romans, the earliest text, includes a quote that pinpoints Jesus' adoption as God's son at resurrection. From Romans, we move backward in Jesus' life to his baptism, which is when Mark declares Jesus' divinity. Then Matthew and Luke move backward still, back to his birth. And lastly, John declares Jesus to be divine at the very beginning of creation. Scholars call this the backward movement theory.

Christ's Bodhi Tree

As for me, I tweak the earliest version of adoptionism, resurrection adoptionism, by connecting it to the crucifixion.. I believe Jesus realized full divinity at his crucifixion. Jesus via his matchless love evidenced on the cross, reached the pinnacle, perfectly revealing the extent of universal love.

Through the crucifixion, Jesus practiced what he preached to the very end and at ultimate cost. The crucifixion showed Jesus' courage amid man's cruelty. It showed his perfect compassion and his dying to save others, namely his disciples and followers, who were at risk of facing the same fate if Jesus chose to violently resist. Jesus took the proverbial bullet of crucifixion for his disciples, whom he called "friends." And what greater love than this, that a man lay down his life for a friend?

His death enabled his disciples to survive to carry on in the work of spreading his message of love. And for us who stand in Jesus' lineage as his disciples and as the church, we have his selfless act to thank—it saved his friends who passed the love on to us, a love that indeed saves. (I discussed this in depth in chapters 10 and 11.)

I think all these things point to this: Jesus' death is the fullest manifestation of his divinity and his ultimate ascension into the divine realm of God's love. Buddhists might call it Christ's *pari-nirvana* moment, his final, ultimate Nirvana. Nirvana literally means extinguishing of suffering. In Jesus' case, we have Nirvana, the extinguishing of suffering, not just for his self but on a collective level. Through his own suffering and death, and his own overcoming of suffering and death, he enables our overcoming of suffering and death. Christ's bodhi tree was the cross, which will, in the end, enlighten us all.

Christ's enlightenment on the cross naturally gave way to his exaltation—his resurrection. Christ's passion and resurrection are fundamental for me, as they are for most Christians. As a Christian, I remember and celebrate Easter along with other Christians.

As for Christmas and Christ's birth and its uniqueness, I celebrate the birth of eternal hope that Christmas represents. I celebrate the image of God born in Jesus. I celebrate the purity of divinity wrapped in the humility of swaddling clothes and lying in a lowly manger. And I celebrate that the purity of divinity never leaves Jesus, that he makes a practice of it throughout his life, and that he carries it all the way to the cross. (Part 1 discusses the story of Christ's birth in depth.)

Part 3

The Wisdom of the Life

— 17 —

Is Jesus the Only Way?

AFTER Jesus' ascension, his earliest followers called their new movement "the Way." The Greek word is *hodos*. *Hodos* means "the road" or "the way," as in, the way bringing us to a destination. The name is inspired by Jesus' frequent use of the word *hodos* in a spiritual way. In the Gospels, Jesus refers to:

- the way of righteousness
- thy way before thee
- the narrow way
- the way of the Lord
- the way of peace
- the way of God

I'd like to focus on this latter example for a bit.

The Way of God

The *hodos* of God is a key phrase in the Yahweh tradition, the faith of Israel, which is the foundation of the early Christian church. Say "the way of God" to a practicing Jew then and now and what comes to mind is Torah, the gift of the Law, the path God wants us to follow.

This notion of the way of God as Torah is important to think about when we consider probably the central passage behind the early title for the church, the Way. That central passage comes from the Gospel of John 14:1–7:

> "Do not let your heart be troubled; have faith in God and have faith in me. In my Father's house there are many places of rest. Would I otherwise have told you that I am going to make a place ready for you? And if I go and make a place ready for you, I am coming again and will take you along with me, so that where I am you might be also. And you know the way to where I am going." Thomas says to him, "Lord, we do not know where you are going. How do we know the way?" Jesus says to him, "I am the way and the truth and the life; no one comes to the Father except through me. If you had known me you would also have recognized my Father. From this moment you know and have seen him."

Let me paraphrase what Jesus is saying here: "You know how in the old days the way to God was the way *of* God, the Torah. You know, take the Law into your heart, into your very being, and follow it, and you will know God and God will know you like he knew Moses? Well," Jesus says, "I am the New Torah. Embodied in me is the way, the truth, the life. If you take me into your heart, into your very being, you will know God and God will know you like he knows me."

The Jesus movement called "the Way" basically submits that Jesus is at one and the same time both the New Torah and the New Moses.

Once Again, Context Matters

It's important to remember a few things when thinking about this central passage. First of all, Jesus is talking to his disciples, to people who've already committed their lives to him, to those who've been following him for some time by this point.

Secondly, Jesus is speaking to one disciple in particular—Thomas. Thomas is the most cognitively minded of the Twelve. He is the kind of guy who is always seeking the logic behind something, always doubting something until he has verifiable evidence. We might say he is a proto-scientist.

Lastly, Jesus is of course speaking pre-crucifixion. This to me is interesting because those who most often point to this verse as absolutely pivotal are those who claim that Jesus' sacrifice on the cross is what it's all about. But that hasn't happened yet. The way that Jesus is, at this point, amounts to his teaching and his exemplifying the way of God. At this point, following

Jesus as the way means following the way of God as taught and modeled *by* Jesus, trusting that this way leads to God. Jesus models the way of God most poignantly and perfectly on the cross, but the cross has not happened yet.

Absolute Way or Relative Way?

I remember being taught in Bible study as a kid how there was a process to Jesus becoming our savior. Until the cross happened, there was a different manner in which Jesus was the way, the truth, and life, one more centered on Jesus as a teacher and model. But when the cross *did* happen, things shifted. The manner in which Jesus is the way, the truth, and the life is his redeeming, substitutiary sacrifice. The pre-crucifixion way no longer applies.

For me, this understanding is faulty. If something is utterly true and absolute at one point in time, it must continue to be true at points of time afterward. If this does not happen, if something that was once true and absolute changes to being no *longer* true or absolute, then it wasn't utterly true or absolute to begin with. It was not absolute truth but relative truth because it changed. For anything that changes is not absolute but relative since it is temporal.

There may be multiple absolute truths that arise in time, but they must arise alongside the pre-existing absolutes already there. There is no such thing as one absolute truth taking the place of another absolute truth. Why? Because if an older absolute truth can be replaced or disappear, it wasn't absolute in the first place. It was temporal. And there is no such thing as a retiring absolute truth. If it was truth and changed, it was a temporal truth not an eternal one.

To see this point, let's ask a question. When Jesus before his crucifixion pointed to himself being the way, the truth, the life, was this essentially and fundamentally true at that very moment? Put in another way, was sincerely following and trusting in Jesus before his crucifixion an ultimate way to God?

Christians everywhere would certainly answer yes to these questions. If so, if the pre-crucified Jesus was the absolute way, truth, and life for people in Jesus' day and following Jesus was then sufficient for salvation, it must remain sufficient. Why? Because absolute truths never go away. Jesus as someone alive teaching his disciples and embodying the way of God is an absolute truth in and of itself. Trusting and following the way of Jesus like his disciples did gets us to God. This is a fundamentally true way then and now.

Variations on the Theme of the Gospel

That there is a pre-crucifixion way, truth, and life and a post-crucifixion way, truth, and life points to a reality I will call variations on the theme of the gospel.

There are three variations on the biblical theme of the gospel. The first variation comes from the Hebrew Bible, the Old Testament to Christians. The second variation comes from the Synoptic Gospels, Matthew, Mark, and Luke. The third comes from Paul as well as the Gospel of John. So we have a BC variation, a DC (during Christ's lifetime) variation, and an AD variation.

Let us look at each of them in turn.

The BC Gospel

In the Hebrew Bible, the gospel, the good news, amounts to God's covenant with an enslaved and oppressed people, Israel. God's covenant with Israel tells the story of God promising faithfulness to and liberation for God's chosen people

The good news is Torah, the Law, the way of God, given by God for the salvation of a people.

This good news of God's salvation through God's covenant is preached and delivered by anointed ones—messiahs, God-anointed kings, literally christs in the plural—and prophets.

But the gospel these messiahs, godly kings, and prophets are preaching is not *their* gospel. It is not the gospel of a messiah or a king or the gospel of a prophet. It is the gospel of *God*. The messiahs, kings, and prophets are merely the messengers, mouthpieces, megaphones of that gospel, preaching about it, informing the people about it, pointing to it. First Chronicles 16:18–23 puts it succinctly:

> "To you I will give the land of Canaan
> as your portion for an inheritance."
> When they were few in number,

> of little account, and strangers in the land,
> wandering from nation to nation,
> from one kingdom to another people,
> he allowed no one to oppress them;
> he rebuked kings on their account,
> saying, "Do not touch my anointed ones;
> do my prophets no harm."
> Sing to the Lord, all the earth.
> Tell of his salvation from day to day.
> (or tell the good news).

In the Hebrew Bible, the gospel means trusting that God is ever present with us and trusting God's covenant with us. It means faith in God's vow to bless us with an inheritance, the inheritance of a home place and the assurance of godly faithfulness toward us. The gospel in the Hebrew Bible in a nutshell is *E-man-u-el*, "God with us." Emanuel here is not a person but a process, a promise, a providence never failing.

The DC Gospel

The second variation on the theme of good news comes to us in the Gospels. It is the DC variation—the During Christ's lifetime variation. Here we are talking about the good news, the gospel found in the Synoptic Gospels—Matthew, Mark, and Luke.

This is the good news preached by Jesus himself during his lifetime. We also see this gospel preached by James, the brother of Jesus, in the New Testament's Epistle of James, who says faith and works go together like two peas in a pod.

Jesus is a new christ, a messiah, an anointed one in the Gospels. He is the Christ for this new eon. In line with the Jewish understanding, Jesus preaches the gospel of God. Jesus never refers to himself as the source of the good news nor the aim of the good news. When Jesus talks about the gospel, he talks repeatedly about and points to the Father and God's kingdom.

The commonwealth of God is the way of heaven brought to earth, where those who are low and humiliated and lost are lifted up and those who are high and proud and the "winners of life" are brought low and to the same plane where God reigns.

The gospel of the commonwealth that Jesus preaches is a gospel that says all will be brought together, all difference, division, and hierarchy expunged, and all will be united under the banner of love.

Jesus is most clear in Luke 4 when he says this:

> "The Spirit of Adonai is upon me;
> therefore he has anointed me
> to announce Good News to the poor;
> he has sent me to proclaim freedom for the imprisoned
> and renewed sight for the blind,
> to release those who have been crushed,
> to proclaim a year of the favor of Adonai." (Complete Jewish Bible)

It›s important to remember that the good news for Jesus is God's doing. The good news for Jesus is that God, with himself as a conduit, is going to return the people of one God to greatness by lifting up the poor and the oppressed.

In these times we live, it is important to note God's definition of greatness. Greatness is defined by lifting up the poor and the oppressed. Want to make a nation great? Lift up the poor and the oppressed.

Jesus certainly sees himself as Messiah, as this age's Messiah, sent to deliver the good news and make real the good news, the good news of God's commonwealth, which will undo the oppression and hierarchy and despair all around. But again, *God* is the point, the *telos*, the end. God's *commonwealth* is the point. Jesus helps us get there. Jesus opens the door to God's commonwealth. Jesus Christ gives a new means to fulfilling Torah. But Jesus' way leads to the Father, not to himself.

In the Gospels, the gospel means trusting God by following Christ and his way of doing justice, loving compassion, and walking with humility.

The AD Gospel

The last variation on the theme of the good news is the one found most clearly in the Gospel of John and in the writings of Paul. This is the AD variation on the gospel.

Paul gives his variation concisely in 1 Corinthians 15:1–4:

> Now I would remind you, brothers and sisters, of the good
> news that I proclaimed to you, which you in turn received, in

> which also you stand, through which also you are being saved, if you hold firmly to the message that I proclaimed to you—unless you have come to believe in vain. For I handed on to you as of first importance what I in turn had received: that Christ died for our sins in accordance with the scriptures, and that he was buried, and that he was raised on the third day in accordance with the scriptures. (NRSV)

Here Paul has tweaked things compared to the gospel Jesus preached. Here we have the gospel not of God alone but of Lord Jesus.

Christ is the means and is included in the end of salvation. Christ is how we get to salvation, and Christ is what we get to at the end of salvation. Before, Christ was merely the means to the end of God; he was the way *to* God, the one who saves us by guiding us to God. By following Jesus, we get to God.

According to traditional interpretations of Paul and John, Christ remains the means to God. Yet Christ is also the aim, the goal, the end, the *telos*. Jesus saves us unto himself.

When we add in the belief that Christ *is* God, the transition from the gospel of God to the gospel of Christ is made complete. The means, the way to get to God, is Christ. What do we get to when we get to God? When we get to God we also get to Christ. Why? Because Christ and God are one.

In Paul, and especially in traditional Christian doctrine, the gospel means trusting Christ. This naturally leads to following him into good works as well, but the sole focus is *sola fide*—only by faith.

A Common Gospel?

So, there are three variations on the theme of the gospel: the BC variation where the good news means following Torah, the way of the one God; the DC variation, where the good news is the commonwealth of God's arrival and our following the way of Messiah Jesus in creating that commonwealth; and the AD variation, where the good news is the salvation of Christ, divine Son of God, and our faith in Christ.

The question is, is there a common denominator? Is there a common strand that unites these three?

What an important question this is. With a common strand we have a more universal gospel, one that unites the gospel of the Hebrew Bible and of the Christian Bible, of the Jew and the Christian.

I say yes, we have a common denominator, a basic gospel. And it is rather simple. It begins with the simple faith claim that God is Love. That is the only faith claim or creed we need. I repeat: God is Love.

That faith being real in our heart, we do as Jesus directly command us to do in Matthew 22. When a Torah expert asked him,

> "Rabbi, which of the mitzvot—commandments—in the Torah is the most important?" Jesus told him, "You are to 'love Adonai your God with all your heart and with all your soul and with all your strength.' This is the greatest and most important mitzvah. And a second is similar to it, 'You are to love your neighbor as yourself.' All of the Torah and the Prophets are dependent on these two." (vv. 36–40, (Complete Jewish Bible)

Love God. Or, God being Love, love Love. Micah 4:3 puts it like this: "Love mercy." Or love compassion.

And in the same way, with the love of God inside us, we are to love neighbor. Love one another. Love others as you love yourself and let justice, flowing out from the source of love, roll down like a mighty water and righteousness like an ever-running stream.

"Even the Atheists?"

I finish this chapter with some thoughts about our atheist brothers and sisters. I've watched in admiration and appreciation Pope Francis discussing this very topic and the very real human beings surrounding it. In his first couple months as pope, Francis gave a homily on the passage from Mark 9:38–40:

> "Teacher," said John, "we saw someone driving out demons in your name and we told him to stop, because he was not one of us."
>
> "Do not stop him," Jesus said. "For no one who does a miracle in my name can in the next moment say anything bad about me, for whoever is not against us is for us.

Preaching on this passage, Francis offered this astonishing statement:

> They complain. "If he is not one of us, he cannot do good. If he is not of our party, he cannot do good." And Jesus corrects them: "Do not hinder him," he says, "let him do good." . . . They were a little intolerant . . . those who do not have the truth, cannot do good . . .

Is Jesus the Only Way?

This was wrong . . . Jesus broadens the horizon. The root of this possibility of doing good—that we all have—is in creation.

The Lord created us in His image and likeness, and we are the image of the Lord, and He does good and all of us have this commandment at heart: do good and do not do evil. All of us. "But, Father, this is not Catholic! He cannot do good." Yes, he can . . . The Lord has redeemed all of us, all of us, with the Blood of Christ: all of us, not just Catholics. Everyone! "Father, the atheists?" Even the atheists. Everyone! . . . We must meet one another doing good. "But I don't believe, Father, I am an atheist!" But do good: we will meet one another there.[1]

Just a couple weeks ago, Pope Francis followed up on this. He did so in such a beautiful, pastoral way that touched many hearts. In fact, this moment of pastoral care gifts us with profound theology.

At a question-and-answer time following a talk by the pope, a young boy named Emanuele, who had just lost his father, had an emotionally wrenching question. Newsweek described it "as a heart-wrenching scene— a young boy approaching the pope, breaking down into tears as onlookers cheer, attempting to encourage the boy."

Unable to get his words out, both sad and afraid, the young boy is called over by the pope. The crying boy, in a quasi-embrace with the pope, speaks in Francis's ears. "The pope shared the exchange with the small crowd, after first asking the child for permission to do."[2]

Here is the transcript of what transpired:

Emanuele: I can't do it!

Pope Francis: Come, come to me, Emanuele! Come to me and whisper it in my ear. Whisper it in my ear. Come, come, come to me.

[Emanuele goes to Pope Francis and whispers his question in his ear]

Pope Francis: If only all of us could cry like Emanuele when we feel sorrow like he does in his heart. He was crying for his dad, and he had the courage to do it before all of us, because he has love for his dad in his heart. I asked Emanuel permission to repeat his question in public, and he said yes. So I'll say it out loud: "A short time ago, my dad died. He was an atheist, but he had all four of his

1. Pope Francis, "Pope at Mass."
2. Marcin, "Pope Francis Hugs, Comforts Little Boy."

children baptized. He was a good man. Is Dad in heaven?" What a beautiful thing, that a son says of his father, "He was good." That man gave a beautiful testimony to his children, for his children to be able to say, "He was a good man." It's a beautiful testimony on the part of the son that he has inherited his dad's strength, and also, that he has had the courage to cry before all of us. If that man was capable of raising children like this, it's true, he was a good man. He was a good man. That man didn't have the gift of faith, he wasn't a believer, but he had his children baptized. He had a good heart. And [Emanuele] is doubting whether or not his dad, not having been a believer, is in Heaven. God is the one who decides who goes to heaven. But how does God's heart react to a Dad like that? How? What do you think? . . . A dad's heart! God has the heart of a father. And faced with a dad, a non-believer, who was able to have his children baptized and to give them that courage, do you think that God would be capable of leaving him far from Him? Do you think so? . . . Say it loudly, with courage . . .

All: No!

Pope Francis: Does God abandon his children?

All: No!

Pope Francis: Does God abandon His children when they are good?

All: No!

Pope Francis: There you go, Emanuele, this is your answer. God surely was proud of your dad, because it's easier to have your children baptized when you are a believer, than to have them baptized when you are not a believer. Surely, this pleased God greatly. Talk with your father, pray to your father. Thank you, Emanuele, for your courage.

We've spoken about his dad, and our dad is God. Let us all pray to our dad, God.

"Our Father . . .".

And now I'll give you the blessing. May every one of you think of the people you love, the people who care about, the people who care about you, and also those we don't like and who are a bit like enemies. Let us pray for them too, so the Lord will bless them too. May He bless all of us and enlighten our heart.[3]

3. Hattrup, "Crying Little Boy Asks Pope."

In this beautiful scene, the pope fleshed out his original words in the first few months of his papacy, the words about atheists and Christians meeting at the good. His conversation with Emanuele pointed to the height and breadth of "the good"—showing humility and compassion. The now deceased father, though expressing unbelief in God, showed us a picture of God by embodying love for his son. God, who is Love, doesn't turn such love away.

So, indeed, let's meet at the good, believers, nonbelievers, and everyone in between. And out of the good, let us strive together to share the good news that self-emptying compassion—the heartbeat of Christ—will save us all.

— 18 —

Isn't the Kingdom of God Theocracy?

> Jesus said therefore, "What is the kingdom of God like? And to what should I compare it? The kingdom of God is like a mustard seed that someone took and sowed in his field; it is the smallest of all the seeds, but when it has grown it is the greatest of shrubs and becomes a tree, so that the birds of the air come and make nests in its branches." (Luke 13:18; Matthew 13:32–33, NRSV)

Every Sunday, churches everywhere join together and pray the Lord's Prayer. We pray, "Thy kingdom come, thy will be done on earth as it is in heaven." The kingdom of God, or as we've been saying, the commonwealth of God, is fundamental to Jesus' self-understanding of the gospel. Simply put, Jesus preached the kingdom of God as the gospel, the good news. Making real the kingdom of God was what moved his ministry and his mission. The church is itself commissioned, first and foremost, to make real the kingdom of God. Christians are a kingdom of God people.

However, in my society and in my time, kingdoms don't really exist, at least not in a non-figurative way. Kings don't rule and reign in America or in the West. What's more, a godly kingdom would be viewed even more suspiciously. A godly kingdom amounts to theocracy. And democracy and theocracy are incongruous.

This begs the question for us in our democracy-loving culture: isn't Jesus calling for a theocracy when he lauds the kingdom of God?

To answer this important question, we have to give a close look at what is meant by the kingdom of God.

Kingdom?

First, let's consider the term "kingdom." Why did Jesus say "kingdom of God" as opposed to, say, "democracy of God"?

Monarchy or some kind of autocracy was the only form of government prevalent at the time Jesus spoke these words. Jesus did not live in a democracy. While there were elements of democracy in the metropolis of Rome, it certainly wasn't full-fledged democracy and it certainly did not move outside the borders of Rome. Rome was an empire, which is monarchy on steroids. Rome occupied Palestine and used a representative monarch, or in other words a puppet king, to rule.

Democracy was unheard of at this point. The only form of government present at the time amounted to the reign of one man at the top ruling over those below.

That definition is important to keep in mind: one man at the top ruling those below.

Of God?

It is essential we understand how Jesus saw God. When we understand how Jesus saw God, we see something profound, even revolutionary. We see that Jesus' kingdom of God is no ordinary kingdom where a figure *at the top* rules those *below*.

Jesus sees God as a father. That's rather straightforward and clear. Jesus' preferred name for God is "Father." God for Jesus is a loving, nurturing, ever-present parent. Such a parent lives with and among his children. Such a parent not only loves his children but shows and shares and expresses that love for and to his children.

What's more, the God Jesus calls Father is present. God as Father is not aloof, nor reigning from a distance, but walking and talking with us, leading us while living in our midst. God as Father is with us, like a ship captain sharing the seas and the storms and guiding us in a close way.

Here's another thing: the system that Jesus calls for, the one that God is the Father of, is one that is radical to even our notions. The system that Jesus prefers is one where there is no hierarchy at all. We see this from Jesus' command that his disciples forget their families.[1]

---

1. Luke 14:25–27.

Why does Jesus command this? Because, like the Roman system, the family system was built on a strict hierarchy. In this case, patriarchy defined the society. Hierarchy by nature lacks equality, as well as empowerment and autonomy for all but the top.

The father in Jesus' culture was the family equivalent of the emperor. The father ruled absolutely, whether he knew best or not. The mother did not even come second in many cases. The oldest son was the next in the hierarchical line. And daughters, well, they were close to invisible.

Jesus, seeing this family system, calls for a complete upending of it. The last shall be first. The least shall be the gauge of how we collectively act. The children shall be the model for godly faith and leadership. The lost, the outsider shall be included. The children shall be exalted and the father humbled.

And where is God in all this? Well, God does not begin at the top. God is not found in the paradigm of *human* father as head. God begins at the bottom, in the last, the least, the lost, and moves upward and outward. God exists at the ground level, as the ground of our being, as the foundation of all of creation, as the floor upon which we stand and receive our purpose. God is a father in the trenches with his family.

Jesus as Proof

Jesus not only preaches this radical view of God, he also practices what he preaches. He embodies this view in his ministry and in his selflessness. Jesus does not hang out with the religious or secular rulers. He doesn't hangout with the respectable fathers in town. He hangs out with the outcasts, the losers, the punks, those whom society has discarded and ignores. He embraces and lauds street kids as the model of greatness and faith. Even his disciples are second-tier citizens—lowly fishermen, merchants, and even the lowliest tax collectors.

The ways Jesus acts and lives, that is how God acts and lives. Jesus is a perfect picture of God. Jesus leads from below, like water finding the lowest level and rising and lifting the lowly up first and all up in the process. As the saying goes, a rising tide lifts all boats. This begins with the lowliest of boats.

God's Kingdom—Proto-Democracy

When Jesus talks about the kingdom of God, he is not talking about some predictable, run-of-the-mill monarchy where God amounts to an extra-kingly and extra-majestic king reigning from the highest place possible. No, Jesus is speaking about something altogether different.

The kingdom of God begins here, now. The kingdom of God begins in the heart, in each of our hearts. "Blessed are the poor in spirit, for theirs is the kingdom." It takes a spirit disposed of any pride and self-importance for the kingdom to be real. The kingdom of God begins with us. I am not saying *God* begins individually with us or any one of us. No, I am saying God's *kingdom* begins with the collective us, with the love that God is in our hearts.

In this way, the kingdom of God is closer to democracy than it is to theocracy. It is not God ruling from on high dictating to those below. It is God ruling at the ground level in us, upward and outward.

God and Heaven

My last point in our discussion of the kingdom of God and why it is not theocracy as we understand it comes from an interchangeable phrase that Jesus uses. It is a telling phrase and helps us to powerfully understand what Jesus is teaching. That interchangeable phrase is "kingdom of heaven."

In fact, we see this interchangeability in different versions of the parable of the mustard seed as found in Matthew, Mark, and Luke. In Mark and Luke, "kingdom of God" is used. In Matthew "kingdom of heaven" is used. The interchangeability of the terms could not be clearer.

"Heaven" is *ouranos* in Greek. As I was told when a boy, heaven is the place where there is no more suffering or sorrow, no more pain or loss, no more separation or discord. Heaven is the place where there are no divides, no discrimination, no inequality, no injustice, no animosity, no hatred, no exclusion. Heaven is the place where we live eternally with God, in complete peace and contentment.

For my son's seventh birthday, I created a playlist of songs incorporating the theme of trains, which he was then fascinated with. Included in the playlist were old gospel songs that used the train as a metaphor for the way leading straight to heaven. In one such gospel song, "Gospel Train," we get a good description of the kingdom of heaven. The last verse says:

> The fare is cheap and all can go
> The rich and poor are there
> No second class aboard this train
> No difference in the fare.

For Jesus, this description is not meant to be a pie-in-the-sky kind of thing. Heaven is our benchmark for earthly life now. "Thy kingdom come, thy will be done on earth as it is in heaven." Thy way of heaven be here and now, O God. That is the prayer.

The Goal: Heaven Here and Now

We live out heaven's kingdom here and now when we live in solidarity with the weakest, the most vulnerable, the most excluded. We live out heaven's kingdom here and now when we allow each person a voice in where we collectively go. We live out heaven's kingdom here and now when we diminish hierarchies of wealth, of power, of influence, of religious faith. We live out heaven's kingdom here and now when we judge less and love more. We live out heaven's kingdom here and now when we give precedence to love and compassion and humility. We live out heaven's kingdom here and now when we work our hardest to make this world a haven of no suffering and sorrow, no pain and loss, no separation and discord as we prepare for heaven to come.

Theocracy means a kingly god dictating and reigning supreme (even over those who define God differently or see no god). But theocracy is not godly. *Ouranocracy*, the rule of heaven, is godly. Letting heaven, the realm of love, reign and rule here and now, this is godly. Making this place we live in as close to heaven for all of us, beginning with the least, the last, the lost—this is godly, as godly as we can get.

Thy commonwealth come, thy will be done, on earth as it is in heaven. Let God's image in each of us be honored, respected, and allowed to guide and discern in our earthly ventures.

— 19 —

Was Jesus Fine with Polytheists?

IN the Gospels, Jesus several times offers up an inclusive approach. The first example we discuss is from Matthew 8. In this story, we see Jesus interact with and applaud the faith of a Roman centurion, who by necessity followed the religion of Rome and the cult of the emperor.

The second example comes from Matthew 15. Here, Jesus interacts with and applauds the faith of a Canaanite woman, which I will discuss in the next chapter. Both the Roman centurion and Canaanite woman were Gentiles.

Before we get to Jesus' interaction with the centurion, I want to clarify the label Gentile. A Gentile is broadly one who does not follow Torah, and thus does not follow the faith of Israel. Because Jesus offered a brand of Torah-following, to be a Gentile would mean you were not a Jesus-follower either at this point. Widening the circle to include Gentiles is something Jesus eventually begins to do in his ministry as the stories we will discuss show. At this point, however, to Jesus' audience, a Gentile is neither a part of the faith of Israel nor of that faith as taught by Jesus.

One more thing. The good works–versus–faith debate that becomes all the rage beginning with Paul is not applicable for Jesus. This debate, which begins with Paul and continues into Augustine and Luther, is in the far-off distance. The good works–versus–faith debate is not a "thing" for Jesus. Jesus wouldn't have understood it.

As an independent rabbi teaching Torah, Jesus saw faith in and following the way of God interchangeably. To be faithful meant exhibiting trust in wisdom teachers and sages guiding you along that way. Faith and following were two sides of the same coin for Jesus. To have one without the other was not possible. As his brother James would later put it, "faith without works is dead," i.e., not alive.

The Story

> On his entry into Capernaum a centurion approached him, imploring him and saying, "Lord, my servant has been laid low in my house, a paralytic, suffering terribly." He says to him, "I shall come and heal him." But in reply the centurion said, "Lord, I am not worthy that you should come in under my roof; but only declare it by a word and my servant will be healed. For I am also a man under authority, having soldiers under me, and to this one I say, 'Go,' and he goes, and to another, 'Come,' and he comes, and to my slave, 'Do this,' and he does it." And, hearing this, Jesus marveled and said to those following him, "Amen, I tell you, I have found no one in Israel with such faith. Moreover, I tell you that many will come from East and West and will recline at table alongside Abraham and Isaac and Jacob in the Kingdom of the heavens; But the sons of the Kingdom will be thrown out into the darkness outside; there will be weeping and grinding of teeth there." And Jesus said to the centurion, "Go; as you have had faith, so let it come to pass for you." And in that hour the servant was healed. (Matthew 8:5–13)

A Roman centurion is presumed to have been a Gentile as well as a polytheist. He was required to vow faithfulness and loyalty to the emperor and Roman religion, at root polytheistic. Roman religion saw the emperor as divine, as the son of god, sometimes even god in the flesh (e.g., Gaius).

A Roman centurion didn't simply take a vow of devotion to the emperor. A centurion was directly engaged in rituals offered to the Roman gods that undergirded the empire and the emperor. The Roman military was in many ways a legion on a crusade to protect and defend the emperor and the religion of Rome.[1]

Master or Mister?

In our story, we have a centurion who comes to Jesus asking that Jesus, as a healer, miraculously cure his servant. This alone is interesting. In the

---

1. Martin, "Gods of the Imperial Roman."

pantheon of gods in Roman religion, there are several related to health and healing, the biggest one being Apollo. Maybe the centurion had tried these gods already, yet healing had not occurred. Maybe the centurion needs something fast and the gods are too slow. Maybe the centurion has decided to forget the Roman gods altogether. We don't know. Nonetheless, he comes to Jesus and seems a bit desperate.

The centurion calls Jesus "lord" or "master." At first blush, one would think this is a sign of allegiance to Jesus, a switching of sides of sorts, a replacing the emperor as lord with Jesus as lord.

This seems unlikely. Greeting someone with the title "lord" (*kyrios* in Greek) doesn't necessarily indicate that a deep conversion to the lordship of Jesus has happened. The title *kyrios* can mean simply "sir" or "mister" in some situations, especially when offered to a stranger. In the least, the centurion in using the honorific *kyrios* is showing Jesus a high level of respect. By asking Jesus what he asks him, the centurion also honors Jesus' spiritual prowess as a healer.

A Humble Warrior

The centurion presents his need. His servant is paralyzed and suffering. This alone is pretty astounding. A centurion showing care for his servant? And in this humble and public way? Indeed, for Jesus this is laudatory. The centurion's sincere concern and advocacy shows a high level of compassion.

Also astounding, we have a respected centurion calling on a religious teacher from the backwaters of Nazareth who just arrived on the scene. The respectable centurion humbly calls this small-town teacher "lord." This same centurion then shows concern for a servant who is suffering with some paralyzing illness.

Jesus, thoroughly impressed, offers his help and healing. "Shall I come to heal the servant?"

The centurion's sense of humility then takes an even profounder step. He declares, "I am not worthy to have you come to my house."

Don't forget he is speaking as a centurion, a respected and feared member of his society. Many Romans would approach the centurion the way the centurion has approached Jesus. His declaration of unworthiness again reveals a high level of humility

The centurion then implicitly compares his role as a leader and head of household with Jesus' role as spiritual healer. He says, "I am also a man under authority." In his work, the centurion, like Jesus, leads people. Both men give direction and their direction is naturally followed. Again, the fact that a centurion, someone given immediate honor and respect and fear when walking into a room, equates himself with an at-this-point common religious teacher from Galilee is further example of the centurion's humility.

Jesus' Favorite Recipe

In the centurion, we have humility toward Jesus combined with compassion for his servant. Humility plus compassion: this is a recipe Jesus absolutely admires and seeks to actualize in all. As the story tells us, Jesus marveled at the centurion's exemplification of godly living.

True godly living amounts to seeing one's inherited privilege and ordained authority and placing them as less important than the underprivileged and powerless. It means placing aside the pride and power of the strongman and seeing the need of a servant caught in an unfair system. It means seeing the worth of an unknown religious teacher born to a subjugated people. It means putting those deemed lowly first, and yourself, deemed highly, second.

Jesus turns to his disciples and followers and tells them, "This is what it looks like to be a follower of God."

Jesus goes on to give a kind of mini-sermon. It is spoken directly to his Torah-following, temple-attending disciples and followers, directly to those standing in the line and faith of Jacob and Judah. And what he says is astounding.

Expanding the Kingdom

Jesus begins by basically saying many will come from the East and West to sit alongside the patriarchs—Abraham, Isaac, Jacob. Who are these people from the East and West? Gentiles. "People from the East and West" is synonymous with Gentiles, non-Judeans. Gentiles "will recline at table alongside Abraham and Isaac and Jacob in the Kingdom of the heavens."

Jesus with these words about Gentiles expands the kingdom, enlarging the house, making the table vastly larger with more seats placed around the table. Gentiles shall sit down next to the revered patriarchs. These new ones seated at the family table are now adopted members of the family, adopted sons and daughters, included in the divine commonwealth. What's more, they are given the best seats in the house, those right next to Abraham, Isaac, and Jacob.

As for the "sons of the kingdom," a phrase meaning the sons and daughters of Israel, those claiming Yahweh, they will be thrown "into outside darkness." Or, they will be placed in the nose-bleed seats.

Jesus is saying the kingdom will follow the example of the centurion. The kingdom will put the lowly first and give them the best seats in the house (next to father Abraham and company). The kingdom will follow the model of making sure the chosen and proud are no longer the center.

Surely, the emotional hurt and discomfort of being "de-centered" produces tears. It produces a figurative grinding of one's teeth as a result of the emotional pain of being separated from God. The psychological darkness that accompanies such a state is beyond hard. However, it is not everlasting.

For Disciples Only

Again, it's important to note that Jesus is talking directly to his Torah-following disciples. His disciples have just begun to follow Jesus. As they begin their journey together, Jesus wants to be clear that the pride of chosenness is nothing to be attached to or rest easy in.

This is to say that with his downgrading of the chosen-ones Jesus is using a teaching method. He is using the threat of an eschatological time-out to put a little fire in his disciples' seats as they begin their new adventure together. He is saying God does not play favorites. God looks at the heart and at evidence of humility and compassion moving in our hands and feet. God wants people to be more like the centurion. And God rewards the good-hearted, the humble and compassionate.

Is the fate of the sons of the kingdom an endless thing? Will their existence in the outer rim away from God and the kingdom be forever and ever? Is Jesus saying absolutely every single son of the kingdom will be cast to the outside darkness beyond the light of Abraham? No. The restoration of the twelve tribes of Israel is presumed for Jesus. Salvation for the ones God brought out of enslavement and forged a sacred covenant with is a given. God is by nature faithful and does not break covenants. Humanity does. Jesus is simply extending chosenness to the Gentile nations, a revolutionary thing to do.

The apostle Paul, writing to the church in Rome a few decades before the Gospel of John was written, has this to say about the children of

Israel: "a partial [i.e., temporary] hardening has happened to Israel, until the fullness of the Gentiles has come in, and so all Israel will be saved" (Rom 11:25–26a).

Jesus is hardening the resolve in his disciples by warning of a sort of incentivizing time-out. The truth Jesus is teaching is that the Gentiles, the so-called non-chosen and lesser-thans, are to be lifted up and given the best seats in the house. But, as Paul tells us, all of Israel is still, in the long-term, safe and will be saved.

In other words, Jesus is not pointing to a superseding and replacing of Israel by faithful Gentiles. Jesus is not tearing down the house and building a new one. Jesus is giving the house—the house of Yahweh—a humungous expansion. And, as a warm welcome, the new family members are given the best and most honored seats at the dinner table. That's what the centurion did. And that's what Jesus has planned.

What Jesus is doing is making the lines around who is chosen and who is unchosen flexible and expansive. Humility and compassion are the key to entering inside that line. In other words, to Jesus, God chooses the humble and the compassionate. Israel was originally chosen on that basis and will remain that way. Now, so will the Gentile nations be.

— 20 —

Did Jesus Really Refer to Gentiles as "Dogs"?

> And going out Jesus departed from there into the regions of Tyre and Sidon. And look: A Canaanite woman from those bounds came forward and cried out, saying, "Have mercy upon me, Lord, son of David, my daughter is badly demon-possessed." But he answered not a word to her. And, approaching, his disciples implored him, saying, "Send her away, for she is crying out behind us." But in reply he said, "I was not sent forth except to the lost sheep of the house of Israel." But she came and prostrated herself to him, saying, "Lord, help me." But in reply he said, "It is not a good thing to take the children's bread and throw it to the dogs." And she said, "Yes, Lord; for the dogs also eat, from the crumbs that fall from their masters' tables." Then in reply Jesus said to her, "O woman, your faith is great; as you desire, so let it happen to you." And her daughter was healed from that hour. (Matthew 15:21–28)

THE story begins with Jesus in Gentile and Samaritan country. Tyre and Sidon are Gentile and Samaritan towns, respectively. Jesus is in this region. The place where the story unfolds matters. That Jesus is in Gentile and Samaritan country is a big surprise and a big tell. Why?

Jesus just a little while ago prohibited his disciples from going into Gentile or Samaritan towns. In Matthew 10:5 he said, "do not go forth on a road of the Gentiles, and do not enter into a city of the Samaritans."

However, in Matthew 15, here are Jesus and his disciples in the Gentile and Samaritan towns of Tyre and Sidon. Somewhere in between Matthew 10 and 15, Jesus had a change of heart.

I suggest a couple things influenced Jesus' change of heart and moved him to become more open to ministry to Gentiles and Samaritans and thus go into Tyre and Sidon. The first influence is the death of John the Baptist in Matthew 13. John the Baptist was not just his cousin but also his mentor and baptizer. Grief like this tends to soften hearts. Like a Samaritan or a Gentile, John was excluded and criticized by the religious-political hierarchy, something that Jesus was increasingly experiencing.

And that is the second point. Jesus is getting more and more flak from the religious hierarchy. We see the religious hierarchy coming down hard on Jesus in the three chapters leading up to Matthew 15.

In Matthew 12, Jesus and his disciples are criticized for not keeping the Sabbath the way the religious hierarchy think it should be kept. He heals on the Sabbath and receives more criticism, which spills over into animosity among the religious hierarchy toward Jesus. A plan is then hatched to "destroy him."

Also, at the end of Matthew 13, Jesus goes to his hometown of Nazareth and is not received well. The religious hierarchy "took offense" and, according to Jesus, he was dishonored.

In the first part of Matthew 15, the religious hierarchy again attack Jesus and his disciples for defiling the "tradition of the elders" and for not following Torah well enough. This seems the final straw for Jesus. He departs the Galilee region and heads for Samaria as if to imply, "Enough is enough. If my people are not going to listen, maybe others will."

In other words, Jesus embodies a command he once gave to his disciples: "When they persecute you in one town, flee to the next." That the next town is in Samaritan or Gentile country no longer matters. Things have changed now.

Changed Mind or Lesson Taught

As for Jesus' interaction with a Canaanite woman in Gentile country, the usual reading of the passage is that the brave Canaanite woman changes Jesus' mind. Upon closer examination, however, the passage shows Jesus teaching his disciples what faith and the commonwealth of faith look like by pointing to the woman's persistent faith.

In the story, Jesus is worn out and needing rest. He heads to Tyre to hide away. Being a "Gentile town," Jesus cannot avoid coming across and interacting with Gentiles. This is what ensues in our story.

Did Jesus Really Refer to Gentiles as "Dogs"?

A Gentile woman pleads that Jesus restore her daughter to psychological and emotional wholeness. Jesus at first doesn't answer her. Again, he is tired and seeking to rest and take a day off. He hopes she will get the idea he needs a break. He also knows he is unlikely to get it.

Jesus' disciples, bothered by her screaming in their ears, "implores" Jesus to stop the madness and "send her away." We know Jesus doesn't take fondly to his disciples imploring him to choose callousness. We have many examples of Jesus' response to this kind of nagging.

Jesus once chastised his disciples for their callousness in trying to turn children away (Matthew 19:14). Jesus once grew bothered by his disciples for imploring him to send hungry people away. He curtly quipped, "You feed them" (Matthew 14:16). Jesus once grew annoyed by his disciples' callousness toward a woman offering him a kind deed, retorting, "Why are you bothering this woman [anointing me with perfume]?" (Matthew 26:10).

Jesus responds to the disciples' imploring him to send the Canaanite woman away by giving a lesson. A lesson for his disciples. Jesus will lift up this Gentile woman and her faith, knowing motherly love never gives up and that she will not go away. He is going to exalt her as a model of faith for his disciples "of little faith." In fact, we might juxtapose the Canaanite woman's faithful persistence despite Jesus' three denials to help her to Peter's fearful persistence in denying Jesus three times in Matthew 26:69–75.

The Test of Jesus' Denials

First, Jesus tests her resilience. Jesus already intuits that her pain and hurt and motherly love and faith are not going to be turned away. Her test is to publicly show that love-soaked faith.

This test is meant for her. It's also meant for his disciples. Jesus wants to show that her faith is so much stronger than the disciples'.

Jesus first ignores her, his first denial. Then he directly denies her initial request with a verbalized denial and rationale. Both denials are a test to the tenacity of her faith.

In the Zen tradition, the first step to entering the monastic life is finding a teacher and proving to that teacher that you won't be turned away. Stories are told of a would-be novice monk being denied and ignored in various ways by a would-be teacher. Rabbi Jesus is doing a version of this, I believe.

In the background of all of this is the fact that Jesus is acting in a way the Pharisees would act. This pharisaical way is evident earlier in Matthew 15. He is also acting in a way the still relatively new disciples might expect any faithful Judean to act toward a Gentile. Jesus is acting in a way Jesus himself claimed was kosher in Matthew 10 (i.e., avoid Gentile and Samaritan regions).

Jesus gives a denial because that is what is expected of a messiah. Any worthy Israelite messiah, according to Jesus' religious culture, is sent forth to the lost sheep of Israel and Israel alone. Basically, Jesus' faux answer mirrors this religious-cultural understanding of what a messiah does. He mirrors that religious-cultural understanding in order to shatter the mirror.

She Persisted

As Jesus intuited, the woman persists. "Lord, help me," she begs. Jesus gives a third denial, once more testing her faith. He gives this rather pointed quip: "It is not good to take the children's bread and throw it to the dogs."

The lost sheep of Israel are the children in his statement. The bread he has come to give is for them. It is the children's bread and no one else's. The "no one else" are called by the euphemism "dogs." Sharp, harsh words coming from Jesus! He doubles down on his Israel-first-and-foremost test.

The Gentile woman's reply is a perfect one and just as pointed. She basically says, "Well, even dogs need to eat, even if it's crumbs from the children's tables." The gist of her response is that Gentiles are people too and need the bread of heaven. She subverts Jesus' euphemism and turns it on its head. It is something Jesus himself is expert at in the Gospels. The Canaanite woman is standing in for Jesus in this moment.

Jesus likes her answer. Her faith passes the test and teaches his disciples in the process. Her faith is a pure model for his disciples to see, the disciples who initially wanted her sent away. Jesus instead engages and exemplifies her. Jesus calls her faith "great." When does he ever say this about his disciples? He grants the Gentile woman her request. He heals her daughter.

The Teaching Moment's Rationale

Why do I think Jesus' conflict with the Gentile woman was a teaching moment? Well, Jesus never resorted to using a euphemism like this (unless he is talking to the religious hierarchy). Jesus' statement seems so out of character otherwise, especially when you compare it to the compassion he shows the Samaritan woman at the well (which we will discuss later).

What's more, if Jesus did not expect to be approached by a Gentile and have to turn her away, why did he go to a Gentile town in the first place? Why not head to the mountains and hills? Jesus expected a Gentile to approach him.

More than this, I believe Jesus was hoping for such a teaching moment. He needed to make it clear that his movement's mission had turned a corner and was heading in a different direction.

By merely going to a Gentile town, Jesus is saying in no uncertain terms just that. He is saying that things have changed now. In Jesus' interaction with the Gentile woman, he makes it plain and confirms things indeed are different now.

Jesus also wants to show the promise and hope in this new mission field to the other, to the dismissed and ignored Gentiles. The Canaanite woman shows this promise and hope perfectly. She perfectly pictures a tenacious faith for the disciples to see. She becomes a lesson of faith, humility, and compassion. In the woman's not being turned around she proves that this new mission field is ripe and ready for the commonwealth's spread.

Confronting Particularism

Alycia McKenzie, professor of homiletics at Perkins School of Theology, suggests this reading of the text. Writing of the parallel text in Mark 7, she writes:

> Jesus spoke as he did, in the mode of rabbinic argumentation, to satirize the attitude of the Pharisees with whom he had just been arguing and to offer a lesson to those around him and the woman. We have no inkling of his facial expression or tone. We do have a record of his pattern of relating to supplicants, and it is with unfailing tenderness and poignancy.[1]

As McKenzie points out, Mark is written for a Gentile Christian audience and seeks "to confront Jewish particularism." What this means is that Jesus is on the "Gentiles' side" in this case. He is confronting the religious exclusivism found in the religious tradition he was born into.

---

1. McKenzie, "Commentary on Mark 7:24–37," pt. 3, para. 3.

A common reading of the text, especially among progressives, is that Jesus basically concedes the point and admits his wrong, learning a lesson himself in the process. This is certainly a fair interpretation, and one I appreciate.

Even with this common interpretation, the confronting of particularism and the focus on pluralism remains. Jesus in the end agrees that the good news of wholeness and healing is not just for the lost sheep of Israel but for all.

Jesus' core message throughout the Gospels adheres to this pluralistic reading of Jesus and the Canaanite woman's interaction. As we saw with Jesus and the centurion, Jesus consistently dismisses attempts to minimize and narrow the reach of God's commonwealth.

— *21* —

Did the Faith of a Group Get Applied to an Individual?

> ... they come bearing a paralytic to him, carried by four men. And, not being able to reach him on account of the crowd, they took away the roof where he was and, having gouged out an opening, they lower the pallet on which the paralytic lay. And Jesus, seeing their faith, says to the paralytic, "Child, your sins are forgiven." But some of the scribes were sitting there and reasoning in their hearts, "Why does this man speak thus? He blasphemes. Who can forgive sins except God alone?" And Jesus, immediately aware in his spirit that they reasoned thus among themselves, says to them, "Why do you reason over these things in your hearts? Which is easier, to say to the paralytic, 'Your sins are forgiven,' or to say, 'Rise and take up your pallet and walk'? But in order that you should know that the Son of Man has power to forgive sins on the earth..."—He says to the paralytic, "I say to you, rise, take up your pallet, and go to your house." And he arose and, immediately taking up the pallet, went out before everyone, so that all were astonished and glorified God, saying, "We have never seen the like." (Mark 2:3–12)

THE story of Jesus healing a paralytic lowered down from an opened roof doesn't explicitly involve someone outside Jesus' religious understanding. From what we gather, all involved are Torah-followers. However, the healing story is interesting because it offers a paradigm where a collective internalizing and externalizing—a collective breathing in and a collective breathing out—of compassion saves an individual from his individual suffering.

The Great Physician Is In and Is Interrupted

Imagine you're Jesus teaching to a large crowd in a house. If you've ever taught, you know how much energy it takes. Deep into his teaching, there is a funny sound, and a hole in the ceiling suddenly develops. Everyone looks up and a group of men are digging a hole in the ceiling made of branches and sapling! Those listening to Jesus stop listening to see what in heavens is going on.

Jesus would have wondered and worried more than anyone about what was happening and what the chaos was about. By this time in Jesus' ministry, he was already being viewed suspiciously. He is already feeling targeted. Maybe Jesus is worried about an attack of some sort. Maybe his time to be arrested and taken away has come.

The Open Roof's Rationale

Making enough space in the ceiling for a man to get through would have taken some time. Jesus' teaching was over as a result. His desire to teach the way of God was now halted. People had to wait. Maybe some left. What was the meaning of all this?

As it turns out, a group of four men have lowered a paralyzed man needing care. We aren't told these four are family or even friends. They could have been strangers for all we know. There seems to be a parallel to the Good Samaritan story, where a stranger sees suffering and gives his time and labor to make sure help is given.

Getting the paralyzed man help and hopefully healing is a group effort. These men expend their time and labor to make this happen. Others expend something for the care of the paralytic as well. The owner of the house with a hole in the ceiling takes a hit, having to repair the roof and ceiling. And of course, there is Jesus, the Great Physician, who is forced to end his teaching prematurely after traveling to be there. Those who traveled to hear Jesus are also denied a full teaching.

This is to say, there is a collective expense to the paralytic man's healing. There is a sharing of the costs to see a stranger healed.

Their Faith, His Healing

In Jesus' day, the accepted idea was that illness was the consequence of some kind of sin, either the sin of the individual who was sick or the sin of his or her parents. While Jesus sometimes rejects this idea (e.g., John 9:3), Jesus acknowledges a link in this case between some kind of wrong choice and the health issue. Maybe the paralytic fell and broke his back after nights of drinking and carousing—I don't know.

Nonetheless, the Great Physician, following the physician's decree, tends to the needs of the person in front of him. The focus for Jesus is bettering people's lives, no matter the cause of their suffering.

One of the most interesting parts of this story comes in verse 5. "Jesus, seeing [the group's] faith, says to the [individual] paralytic, 'Child, your sins are forgiven.'"

Because of the collective faith and compassion of the four men, *as well as* Jesus' faithful and compassionate response, the individual paralytic's sins are forgiven and healing happens. The collective faith and compassion of the four men gives way to Jesus' faith and compassion and together they establish a paradigm for healing and wholeness.

Embodied Compassion Saves

We see the same paradigm in the example of the two Gentiles we already talked about—the centurion and the Gentile woman. Like the four men lowering down the paralytic, the centurion and Gentile woman didn't heal anyone—Jesus did that—but their compassion was an essential link in the chain. *Jesus* healed the centurion's servant and the Gentile woman's daughter *after* the centurion and Gentile woman's compassionate acts pointed to the need.

We have three steps here. Step 1: compassion moves the ones who bring the suffering to Jesus' attention and in turn moves Jesus. Step 2: Jesus, being divine, embodies all compassion, including the compassion all around him and in those coming to him. Step 3: earthly and heavenly compassion unites, transform all involved, and healing and salvation results.

Again, Jesus and those who brought suffering souls to him shared something essential. They shared compassion. And this collective compassion, embodied in Jesus, led to forgiveness and salvation via Jesus' climatic act.

This paradigm of collective compassion internalized and embodied in Christ is essential. We see the paradigm most clearly in the cross, as we've discussed.

— 22 —

What's the Difference between Humility and Humiliation?

"Blessed are you who are poor,
for yours is the kingdom of God . . .
But woe to you who are rich,
for you have already received your comfort." (Luke 6:20, 24, NIV)

"All those who exalt themselves will be humbled, and those who humble themselves will be exalted." (Luke 14:11, NIV)

"So the last will be first, and the first will be last." (Matthew 20:16, NIV)

It is clear that Jesus and the Christian faith as a whole call for followers to humble themselves. Being selfless and self-emptying is central to the Christian life.

However, what about those who feel continually humiliated by circumstances, by the structure of society, by the predicament of their life? What about those people whose self already feels so empty, who give so much they have nothing left? What about those among us who give and give and give without stopping to refuel or receive?

The Humble by Circumstance

I begin with those who feel humiliated by life from the get-go, who feel stomped on, forgotten about, and even despised for no other reason than being born. How can you ask someone perennially humiliated to embrace humility?

In Jesus' time, there was a category of people defined by the fact they were excluded from the greater society. They are often called "sinners" in the Gospels. We might translate "sinners" as "the already humiliated."

Included in the category of "sinner" in Jesus' religious culture were Gentiles. Gentiles didn't follow Torah, engage in purification rituals, or eat kosher.

Eating kosher is particularly relevant here. The Gospels regularly show Jesus eating with the so-called sinners. Jesus' fellow diners in this case are not eating kosher and may be serving *him* non-kosher! Jesus dining with non-kosher-eating and -serving Gentiles is a tremendous example of Jesus meeting people where they are without judgment. However, it was regarded as blatantly breaking kosher regulations.

In Jesus' culture, dining with someone was a very significant act. To dine with someone meant to declare a level of closeness and intimacy that neared the level of family. Dining in ancient Palestinian culture, as now in many ways, was a kind of sacred event. Jesus dining with sinners and tax-collectors was a *huge* deal to a religious culture hyper-focused on issues of purity and external signs of holiness.

Beyond a Sinner

Another category of people on the "already humiliated" list are the tax-collectors. To call someone a "tax collector" was the equivalent of a euphemism. It was kind of like calling someone a "mobster." It was not exactly a complement.

Tax collectors were Jews who worked for Rome, basically. They collected taxes and handed these off to Rome. What's more, they worked for Rome and made a profit from it, skimming off the top of the monies given them.

They were given a special place in the hierarchy of sinners. A common phrase in the Gospels is "the tax collectors and the sinners." The tax collectors were seen as worse than "sinners." They were in a category all their own. They were seen as the hands of the devil, as traitors. They were demonized more than any other group.

It is amazing in and of itself that Jesus chooses to call Matthew, a tax collector, as one of his disciples.

In Matthew 9:9-12 we read:

> As Jesus went on from there, he saw a man named Matthew sitting at the tax collector's booth. "Follow me," he told him, and Matthew got up and followed him.
> While Jesus was having dinner at Matthew's house, many tax collectors and sinners came and ate with him and his disciples. When the Pharisees saw this, they asked his disciples, "Why does your teacher eat with tax collectors and sinners?"
> On hearing this, Jesus said, "It is not the healthy who need a doctor, but the sick. But go and learn what this means: 'I desire mercy, not sacrifice.' For I have not come to call the righteous, but sinners."

That Jesus calls a tax collector to be one of the Twelve tells us Jesus sought to include all, beginning with those humiliated by the reality on the ground, by a system that ignores them, rejects them, or creates them. (The tax collectors are in this latter group, created by Rome.) Jesus is positing a new teaching, a new way of faith, a new world order, one that includes at the top the despised, the demonized, and the humiliated, all transformed or transforming.

Relationship First

We learn something else from Jesus calling Matthew as his disciple. A changed life, a transformed life from the start, is not necessarily a prerequisite for Jesus. For the already humiliated among us, for the despised and demonized among us, Jesus includes them, accepts them right away. He doesn't mandate faith in them. He includes them and allows them to start the process that *leads* to a changed life. Including them without first mandating repentance is a grace-soaked caveat. It is a caveat that amounts to the first step in the process of transformation, both in them and in society.

In the case of the already humiliated, Jesus reaches out, says "follow me," and creates a relationship. Within this process of relationship, a changed life happens. Jesus asks Matthew to join the band and Jesus begins walking and talking with him. As a result of Jesus reaching out and including Matthew, as a result of *relationship*, Matthew's heart is transformed, and the commonwealth of God gets one more brick in its building.

Jesus requires humility, that is clear. For those already made humble by the power structure, for people like tax collectors and prostitutes, the requirement of humility is naturally met. Jesus then requires relationship. He requires walking in the way of love in relationship and community. Transformation overflows from that.

Or Humility First

For those proud, powerful, and wealthy; for those who *don't* know or have forgotten what it feels like to be hated and humiliated; what's more, for those who *do* the humiliating and humiliate others, the prerequisites are different. A heart of humility needs to be made evident first.

We see this in the story of Zacchaeus. It is found in Luke 19:1–10:

> Jesus entered Jericho and was passing through. A man was there by the name of Zacchaeus; he was a chief tax collector and was wealthy. He wanted to see who Jesus was, but because he was short he could not see over the crowd. So he ran ahead and climbed a sycamore-figtree to see him, since Jesus was coming that way.
>
> When Jesus reached the spot, he looked up and said to him, "Zacchaeus, come down immediately. I must stay at your house today." So he came down at once and welcomed him gladly. All the people saw this and began to mutter, "He has gone to be the guest of a sinner."
>
> But Zacchaeus stood up and said to the Lord, "Look, Lord! Here and now I give half of my possessions to the poor, and if I have cheated anybody out of anything, I will pay back four times the amount.
>
> Jesus said to him, "Today salvation has come to this house, because this man, too, is a son of Abraham. For the Son of Man came to seek and to save the lost."

Compared to Matthew, Zacchaeus has it good. Matthew is akin to your basic IRS agent, your basic low-level IRS grunt who has to do the dirty work of making phone calls and facing hostile people being audited and being asked to send in their check. Matthew was humiliated daily.

Zacchaeus was akin to the director of the IRS. He was the chief and was fortunate enough to be above it all. And he was wealthy as a result.

We often read about Zacchaeus being small in stature and it prompts sympathy in us. "Poor guy. He is so small he has to climb a tree to see Jesus." But prompting sympathy for short people is not the point of the story, nor is the fact that Zacchaeus is small. He is small in stature but large in status.

Zacchaeus is rich and powerful, and he has gotten there through the small and treacherous task of being chief henchman for the oppressor.

He climbs the tree not just to see but to be inconspicuous, to hide. He is too proud and powerful to be seen pushing through the crowd and getting right up front, right before Jesus. The people know who the chief of the tax collectors is. He's easily recognized. He'd be seen, found out, discovered by being up front. So he instead hides by climbing a tree.

No More Hiding

Humility is missing in Zacchaeus, in other words. At least, until he is called out.

Jesus humbles him right then and there. He points him out sitting in that tree. It's as if Jesus is saying, "Chief of tax collectors sitting in a tree, H-I-D-I-N-G."

Then Jesus heightens the embarrassment. "I, a lowly carpenter and now spiritual teacher from a small, know-nothing town, am going to come make a house call to your beautiful house in the suburbs tonight."

The story ends with restorative justice. In order to follow Jesus, Zaccheus gives half of his possessions to the poor and four times what he wrongfully took in his work.

This is completely in line with what Jesus says and does elsewhere. To the rich man in Matthew 19 Jesus said, "if you want to follow me, first sell your possessions and give the money to the poor." In other words, Jesus says, "show me you are humble enough to follow and be transformed." Jesus goes onto say, "it is hard for a rich man to enter the kingdom heaven, as hard as a camel entering the eye of a pin-needle."

Or Compassion Always

Humility comes first. If it's there already, then you are good, you can follow. If it's *not* there, then it first needs to be.

Humility leads to followship and fellowship and then to transformation; that is the order of things for Jesus.

There are those who feel continually humiliated by life. Then there are those who live lives of wealth, status, and pride. But what about those in the middle? What about those who live relatively good lives? They work hard but do not know wealth or status or pride.

Well, humility is still required. Humility in this case comes in the form of empathy and compassion, where we seek to feel the pain of the other and seek to help.

Selflessness or Self-Care?

Often, when we talk about humility, the concern arises of taking humility too far. If we put others first all the time and forget about ourselves and about caring for ourselves, we risk ignoring ourselves and our needs. I think this is a legitimate concern. I think of my mother, who had six children and worked so hard giving of herself. She was always on the verge of burnout. This is to say, self-care is important.

But we must be clear: self-care is an example of humility. It amounts to being humble enough to admit we need help, that we can't keep doing it all and all alone. It is being humble enough to say, "I need to stop and receive care instead of always giving it. I need to go to a massage therapist. I need to go to yoga and learn yoga from a teacher. I need to take a break and get tea with a friend. I need to take a walk in the woods and have the woods reinvigorate me. I need to pray and meditate where I regularly seek God's help and stop doing, doing, doing, and just be with God. I need something beyond just self."

The exemplars of humility for Jesus are children. Children are the chiefs of humility. And children innately know they need help, that they can't do it all, that they need to receive care, that they need others, namely their parents.

In other words, humility is not self-punishment, it is not masochism. We are to be humble enough to love neighbor as ourselves. And we need to love ourselves in order to love others. It is just that the love of ourselves should not be far and above our love of others. If I love myself so much that I ignore others' pain and hurt and needs, I am getting into the realm of selfishness and pride. And that is a dangerous place to be.

— 23 —

Did Jesus Give a Call to Arms?

"Do not think that I have come to bring peace to the earth; I have not come to bring peace, but a sword." (Matthew 10:34)

It is interesting how we humans so easily put people we adore on a pedestal. We see them as so good, so kind, so perfect, that it becomes hard for us to see any room to grow, to gain new insights, to progress in the way of peace.

When we do this, though, we in truth rob our heroes of their humanity. We take their humanness from them. We make a caricature of them—the perfect man or woman, one who is so divine that growth is a non-starter.

This is especially true when it comes to religious figures. We declare people saints. Superhuman. We forget to see *persons*, persons full of complexity with a mix of emotions and evolution. We forget religious figures and founders are more like us than not. In their life they too progressed and matured and got better.

This applies even to Jesus. Like God as pictured in the Old Testament, Jesus was influenced by his context and by the people around him. He could gain new insight, ponder things, and even change his mind. I think this is one way to make sense of Jesus' words in Matthew 10:34.

Bring a Sword or Put It Away?

Jesus says these words from Matthew 10:34 at the very beginning of his ministry. Just a few verses early, in Matthew 10:1–2, Jesus is choosing his twelve disciples. Jesus is just finding his way at the beginning of his ministry.

By the time Matthew 26 comes around, three or so years later, something has changed in Jesus. The same man who said "I have come bringing a sword" in Matthew 10 says in Matthew 26:52 something very different: "Put the sword away. He who lives by the sword shall die by the sword."

Jesus says these words to his closest disciple Peter after Peter drew his sword and struck the ear of a servant. Somewhere along the road, between Matthew 10 and Matthew 26, Jesus chose the path of unequivocal nonviolence.

This recalls Dr. King. Early in his leadership of the civil rights movement, during the Montgomery bus boycott of 1956, he had guards with guns standing watch in front of his house. But just a few years later, after he committed himself to the path of nonviolence as taught by Gandhi, he had his guards put their guns away.

Jesus seemingly changing his mind also recalls the famous story of Noah and the Ark. God went from globally wiping out a world of sinners to promising never to take such drastic and destructive measures again, implying that he regretted such actions.

There is hope for all of us. It is never too late to gain new insights, ponder things, and experience a change of heart. It is never too late for us to grow into the path of peace.

No Justice, No Peace

There's another way to look at Matthew 10:34 that also can teach us a great deal.

When Jesus says," I've come not to bring peace," he is talking about a specific kind of peace. The kind of peace Jesus says he's *not* about, the kind of peace that Jesus says he has *not* come to bring, is a shallow peace. The peace Jesus could do without is a peace that is simply an absence of conflict.

Sometimes conflict is needed. There are some wrongs in life that make it unavoidable. There are some wrongs we must confront, wielding the sword of love. Only by confronting these wrongs can true peace ever be realized in a deep way.

And Jesus is referring to such an avoidable wrong in Matthew 10. It is a systemic wrong. The wrong of social inequality and rigid hierarchy where the respected and powerful are high, secure, and comfortable and everyone else is far below, unprotected and struggling. A peace built on this, where the powerful maintain a fake peace through fear and intimidation and pulling the strings of power, is not the kind of peace Jesus is about or has come to offer.

Jesus wants a peace based in justice, equality, and fairness. Jesus called for an egalitarian peace, not one based in power. The peace Jesus wants is one built on a social equilibrium where the poor and the weak are lifted up and the rich and the powerful are brought to a more even plain. An unjust peace is no peace at all for Jesus. No justice, no peace.

Battling What Holds Us Back

But we can also apply Jesus' avoidance of quick and easy peace to inner peace. We all want inner peace. It is certainly something we should strive for. However, what if getting at true peace means first confronting some things in our lives? What if getting to inner peace requires doing inner battle with our anger, our sadness, our prejudices, our attachments, our hatreds? What if inner peace involves taking the sword of love and felling all the obstacles holding us back?

Yes, sometimes we need to be gentle on ourselves. Sometimes we need to forgive ourselves and look past certain things in ourselves. Sometimes we need to focus on the kingdom of God within us. But not at the expense of staying stuck or ignoring reality.

Other times, it is necessary to confront negative habits, a paralyzing past, destructive tendencies, or social wrongs we are unconsciously part of. Confronting ourselves with brutal honesty is sometimes a necessary step to finding real and lasting inner peace. Internal struggle is sometimes part of the process to realizing internal peace.

That is what I think Jesus is trying to say to us by his still very provocative and counterintuitive statement. Without the strenuous internal work, peace is an illusion and not worthy of being brought.

— 24 —

Was Jesus Anti-Family?

"For I have come to turn
'a man against his father,
a daughter against her mother,
a daughter-in-law against her mother-in-law—
a man's enemies will be the members of his own household.'
Anyone who loves their father or mother more than me is not worthy of me; anyone who loves their son or daughter more than me is not worthy of me." (Matthew 10:35–38, NRSV)

From an initial reading, Jesus' take on the family in Matthew 10 seems rather harsh, doesn't it? Jesus seems to be dismissing family values. In fact, he seems to be condemning family values. He seems out to destroy families. In the least, he seems out to divide families. So much for family values. What is this about?

Well, let's delve deeper and examine what Jesus is really criticizing. As it turns out, it's something he criticizes a great deal in the Gospels.

Family as a Pyramid Scheme

Ancient Palestinian social and economic systems were strictly hierarchical and tiered sort of like a pyramid scheme. A pyramid scheme has one guy seated at the top, in control, in power, and holding the wealth. Those below earn money, obtain power, or gather resources, but a big portion of all these things go to and through the man at the top first. More levels of people inevitably develop below. But the money, power, and resources keeps flowing upward, into the pockets of those above, with a great deal of the money going into the pockets of the big guy at the very top. It is sort of trickle-down economics in reverse. Most of the money made at the bottom flows back up, filling the coffers of those above.

This kind of pyramid scheme is everywhere in Jesus' time. It is a society-wide phenomenon.

The result is rigid, institutionalized hierarchy. The society-wide pyramid scheme instills a huge divide between those at the top and those below. In ancient Palestine, the big man upstairs is the emperor. And there is a clear line between the top and the levels below. And whatever power, wealth, or betterment there is to be had, a big portion flows upward to the top in Rome.

This structure applies even to the family system in ancient Palestine. In fact, it starts in the family. The father rules the roost. It is a heavily patriarchal society. The father is the king in the family. The mother is well below, followed just a little bit in the order of things by the firstborn son. Younger sons follow in the hierarchal line. Then the oldest sister and younger sisters. At the very bottom are daughters-in-law, beginning with the one who marries the oldest son and lives with the immediate family.

This is the style of family Jesus is referring to in Matthew 10. And Jesus deplores this setup. He deplores it so much that he wants to topple it. He wants to turn things on their head and upend the pyramid. And he calls on his disciples to join him in this toppling, in this upending.

New Paradigm over Old Pyramids

Jesus talked over and over again about a new paradigm. Jesus taught a new paradigm to completely replace the old pyramid schemes. It is a new paradigm of the commonwealth of God.

This new paradigm begins with God as Father. And as Father, God is not above but with those at the bottom.

We should be clear: the "Father God" Jesus shows us is unlike the fathers defined by his culture. In fact, Jesus shows us a Father God who is countercultural. This Father God possesses motherly qualities. This Father God, according to Jesus, is as feminine as he is masculine by his culture's standards.

This was revolutionary to those listening to Jesus. It is no wonder the religious authorities were shocked and offended. The way Jesus referred to God as Father, as a father with an intrinsic maternal way of being, was a shock to the religious system.

This God comes down to the humblest levels of society and lifts up the lowest, the least, and last. This God comes down to earth to topple and crush the pyramids, crush the pyramids into a road leading to the commonwealth of God, a commonwealth marked by equality among all, justice for all, and compassion toward all.

The toppling that Jesus beckons must happen from top to bottom. This toppling means the traditional family system is upended. The children shall lead. Jesus has come to turn the traditional family system, based on rigid hierarchy and a pyramid scheme-like approach, on its head.

Love as the Center

The aim of upending the family system is that love itself becomes the center of the home. The aim is family life built on the equilibrium and equalizer of love, godly love.

In this new paradigm, Father-Mother comes down to the children's level and collaborates to create a new way. Children are no longer obliged to adorn the patriarch with extreme deference and fear but instead look to the reality of a loving relationship with their parents for meaning and purpose. And out of relationship, honor and respect naturally comes. Even mother and daughter-in-law join hands and throw the letter of the law away for the spirit of love.

Jesus envisions a beloved community, beginning with a new way of doing family and moving outward, a beloved community where all meet at the center of love, where God equalizes and evens out all disparities and divisions, where authority is shared and collaboration is a way of life, even between parent and children.

Forget Your Parents?

I close with maybe the most difficult verses of Matthew 10, verses 37–38, where Jesus says, "If you love your parents or your children more than me, you are not worthy of me."

The love Jesus wants his disciples to generally embody and live out is not a sentimental, attachment sort of love. The kind of love Jesus wants us to show is the love that God shows. Jesus wants us to love others, including our parents and our children, with the kind of love that God loves *us* with.

The love that God loves us with is known as *agape* love. It is an eternal, unconditional love, the profoundest love marked by grace and forgiveness, by tenderness and tenacity. It is a love that knows no greater or lesser, no more or no less. It is a love that knows no boundaries.

If we love our parents and our children with this kind of love, with *agape* love, and we love Jesus with *agape* love, it is the *same* love. With such a love there is no ranking or rank. The love for parent, child, and Jesus comes from the same divine source, and it has the same aim. In participating in godly, *agape* love for our family, we practice the way of love and love God in the process.

So, at the essential level of *agape* love there is no loving anyone more than another. With *agape* love, there is no loving father or child more than loving our teacher Jesus. Love for parent or child, if a godly love, partakes of the same love shown for Christ or for God. There is just one love, and the loving of another with this one love. That is the goal a disciple of Jesus should have and seek after, a love that makes equality, justice, and compassion real.

Will such a love ever be perfected in us? Not in this life. Will we naturally love our parents and especially our children more than we love an abstract idea of God? Of course. But know this: the journey of loving one another with the one love of God, that *is* the singular destination. The better we love our parents and our children, the better we practice the way of *agape* love and in turn love God. We must begin the practice of agape love somewhere. What better place to begin than in loving parent and children with the love of God? For there is one Love and it works through all the universe and in our loving of another.

— 25 —

Did Jesus Make a Heretic His People's Teacher

JESUS grew up in a very religious culture. His culture was defined by the Yahweh-Torah tradition. The patriarchs and prophets were part of the soil of his community and his people. The understanding of God as singular and personal was engrained in the spiritual food of the people.

To the religiously correct, to the orthodox of his community, Samaritans were heretics. They were heretics who lived next door but excluded.. And because they lived right next door (across the invisible border), and interactions were unavoidable, conflict and othering was unavoidable. Samaritans were often seen as not just religiously wrong but as wholly the enemy.

For us to understand what this means, we must understand the Samaritan religion. So, let me delve into the religious understanding and teachings of the Samaritans.

Who Are the Samaritans?

I begin my discussion of the Samaritans by saying, the Samaritans are still around, albeit in very small numbers—only 750 or so remain in the Tel Aviv area of Israel. Hence, past and present tenses are used interchangeably below.

The historic roots of the Samaritan people are not completely understood. There is much debate regarding how the Samaritans came to be. One view, the view long held by the Jewish tradition, is that the Samaritans originated during the time of the Babylonian captivity, which occurred nearly six hundred years before Christ. Jews were exiled from Israel and scattered throughout the world. The Babylonians, needing workers, brought in people from Samaria, a location east of Israel.

After the Jews returned from their two hundred years of exile, they encountered the Samaritans inhabiting what they saw as "their land." Sounds familiar, doesn't it? And as with Jews returning to Israel in the mid-1900s to find Palestinians there, tension and conflict ensued between the Samaritans and Jews and would continue for hundreds of years.

The idea that Samaritans and Jews developed as distinct peoples brought together post-exile is increasingly being questioned and rejected. More probing studies of religious texts and archeological discoveries have led many scholars to argue that the Jews and the Samaritans are ethnically related.

As genomic biologist Anne Wojnicki states:

> Researchers argue that during the Babylonian Captivity, not all Jews were rounded up and sent away. Some Jews stayed behind, possibly marrying other groups brought in to the area, like those brought in from Samaria. This would make sense given that, even though Samaritans are not considered Jews, they share many of the same ancient Hebrew rituals. While these rituals have evolved for hundreds of years among most Jewish sects we know of, they remain unchanged among the isolated Samaritans, even to this day.[1]

There have been a number of recent genetic studies of the Samaritans. These studies have made it clear that Jews and Samaritans share a common ancestry, probably within the last few thousand years.

Biblical Differences

That said, there are theological differences that separate the two groups. The Samaritan Bible, first of all, is different. The Samaritan Bible is written in the Samaritan alphabet and is called the Samaritan Pentateuch or the Samaritan Torah. There are many minor differences, nearly six thousand, between the Samaritan Torah and the Hebrew Torah.

There are major differences as well. First of all, the Samaritan Bible only includes the first five books, the Pentateuch—Genesis, Exodus,

---

1. Wojnicki, "More than Just a Parable," para. 5.

Leviticus, Numbers, Deuteronomy. No Psalms, no Proverbs, no books of Jeremiah or Isaiah, etc. Just the Pentateuch.

Another major difference between the Samaritans and the Jews involves sacred space. The Samaritan Torah states Mount Gerizim is at the center of the world. God, after giving the Ten Commandments to his chosen people, commands the construction of an altar for all sacrifices to God on Mount Gerizim, which is near the Jordan River.

Mount Gerizim, located in the modern-day West Bank, is the Samaritans' *axis mundi*. Jews look some forty-six miles south, to Mount Zion and Jerusalem, and see it as the *axis mundi*, the center of the world.

Theological Differences

Maybe the most significant variance in the Samaritan Torah is its view of God. The Samaritan text is marked by less anthropomorphic language. In other words, it doesn't ascribe to God many humanlike characteristics or humanlike actions. Here are some examples of these variations.

In Exodus 15:8, the Hebrew text refers to God's breath coming from nostrils as if God literally has nostrils. The Samaritan text of Exodus 15:8 refers to breath coming simply from God without reference to human anatomy.

And in Deuteronomy 32:6, the Hebrew text has God referred to as Father. Like doxologies in more progressive churches that replace the gender-exclusive term Father with Creator, the Samaritan text uses Creator instead of Father.

Lastly, instead of describing Yahweh as directly interacting with—meeting, speaking with—humans face to face as we see in the Hebrew text, the Samaritan text has the angel of Yahweh doing this direct interacting with humans. God is too transcendent and ineffable to directly interact with humans.

These differences show how the Samaritan Torah and belief system saw God. The Samaritans see God as more transcendent, more universal and less imminent, less here and now, less earthly, less humanlike. The Samaritan God is holy other and unknowable. The Samaritans highlight and consistently align their own scripture with Numbers 23:19 "God is not human, that he should lie, not a human being, that changes his mind."

A Reminder

Before we get to Jesus' most famous parable, I want to again highlight that in Jesus' time Samaritans and Jews were mortal enemies. The religious hierarchy of the Jewish and Samaritan traditions preached complete segregation between the two groups. Think Jim Crow–era segregation, where it would be very dangerous for a Black person to enter a segregated area of town or place of commerce. For the Samaritans and Jews, even having a conversation was to be strictly avoided. This presumes animosity. And often this animosity led to outright violence. The ancient Palestine historian Josephus reports this happening on several occasions, in fact.

With this understood, Jesus highlighting a Samaritan as hero was itself rather radical in Jesus' context.

Parable, Explained

Here is Jesus' ageless parable of the Good Samaritan:

> But he, wishing to vindicate himself, said to Jesus, "And who is my neighbor?" Taking this up, Jesus said, "A certain man was going down from Jerusalem, and he fell among bandits, who stripped him and rained blows upon him and went away leaving him half dead. And by a coincidence a certain priest was going down by that road and, seeing him, passed by on the opposite side. And a Levite also, coming upon the place and seeing him, passed by on the opposite side. But a certain Samaritan on a journey came upon him and was inwardly moved with compassion, And approaching bandaged his wounds, pouring on oil and wine, and setting him upon his own mount he brought him to a lodge and cared for him. And taking out two denarii on the following day he gave them to the keeper of the lodge and said, 'Take care of him, and whatever you spend beyond this I shall repay you on my return.' Who of these three does it seem to you became a neighbor to the man falling among bandits?" And he said, "The one treating him with mercy." And Jesus said to him, "Go and do likewise."

Jesus with the parable of the Good Samaritan teaches this: don't ask who your neighbor is so you can be neighborly to them, ask *how* you can be a neighbor to whomever?.

Jesus is also teaching in the parable that compassionate neighborliness toward all indicates love of God. One leads into the other. Love of God accompanies love of neighbor. To know life in the realm of the commonwealth of God means both love for God and love of neighbor.

What stands out in the parable is that Jesus has the exemplar of humility and compassion be a Samaritan. In Jesus' context, having a Samaritan be the exemplar, the hero, is scandalous to his listeners' ears.

As we've discussed, the Samaritans weren't some generic group in the neighborhood. Referring to the Samaritans wasn't like referring to the Italians down the street or the Swedish couple next door. Samaritans were excluded from the neighborhood. Jesus was sort of saying to Sunni Muslims, "This Shia Muslim is the prime example of faith and faithfulness for you Sunni Muslims." Jesus was saying, "Evangelical Christian, this gay agnostic is the prime example of Christian goodness and compassion." Or to an Israeli, "This Palestinian is the prime example of following Torah."

Jesus' Un-Samaritan Theology

Jesus' inclusion of the Samaritan is especially noteworthy because Samaritan theology profoundly counters his own. Jesus' fatherly-God-based theology to a great degree opposes Samaritan theology. Jesus disagreed with the Samaritans even more than the Jewish clergy he is talking to and sharing the parable with.

As we've looked at before, Jesus' preferred image for and understanding of God is Father. This was uncommon in his day, especially for Jewish clergy. He especially would have not have liked the Samaritans changing Father to Creator. God for Jesus was imminent, on earth, here, now, with us like a good father is with his child, within us like a father's love is within his child's heart, not just transcendent and distant from us.

Nonetheless, Jesus points to a Samaritan as the exemplar of the faith and faith practice. He is saying, "Yes, you may see them as your mortal enemy. Yes, they practice their faith differently and view God differently. Yes, their theology is wholly different, especially from mine. But they still can epitomize and embody what it means to be a follower of Torah." Jesus is saying to the religious clergy that compassion matters most, even more than difference. For compassion transcends differences, even theological ones. Compassion overrides difference, be it religious, cultural, or racial. For it is compassion that transforms us and saves us.

The Good Heretic?

Back to this chapter's key question. Did Jesus make a heretic his people's teacher? If you see Samaritans as heretics, then the answer cannot be avoided. Yes, Jesus made a heretic the lesson of the story. But this begs another question: did Jesus believe Samaritans were heretics?

I don't believe Jesus saw Samaritans as heretical. I think he saw the Samaritan faith as a viable option. Why? Because he saw that Samaritan faith produce the fruit of humility and compassion. And as we've seen, for Jesus there is nothing more important than the fruit of humility and compassion. It's more important than chosen status, religious orthodoxy, or theological conformity.

Jesus focused more on orthopraxis than orthodoxy. Orthopraxis translates as correct practice. For Jesus, it mattered more that one practice self-emptying compassion than that one assert a particular theological worldview. Whether you are a traditional Judean Torah-follower, a Samaritan mystic, or a Gentile polytheist, if humility and compassion are operating principles evidenced in your life, Jesus is satisfied and says, "Follow me."

For Jesus, the tree of faith and the fruit of that tree are inextricably connected. The difference between an acceptable tree of faith and an unacceptable one is the fruit of that tree. If a tree produces no fruit, then that tree is useless for the commonwealth and hence unacceptable. If a tree produces fruit but it is inedible or poisonous, then that tree is useless or even harmful and hence unacceptable as well. On the other hand, if a tree of faith produces good fruit that benefits the commonwealth, then it is acceptable.

It's important to note that Jesus does not give up on such "fruitless trees." Luke 13:8 shows Jesus tending to such fruitlessness even though it is a problem. But the commonwealth demands fruitfulness, so the nutrient of fruit can be shared.

The Good Samaritan's faith produced the humble and compassionate act of caring for a stranger. That faith cannot be seen as other than acceptable and viable. It is the "good in, good out" principle at work. Thus, Jesus does not condemn the Samaritan faith but lauds the faithful Samaritan's actions. Such actions help foster and build God's commonwealth. And building the commonwealth is the point. We should be careful to note that Jesus' inclusivity does not mean he ignores difference. We see clearly in the next chapter how Jesus acknowledges difference. But for Jesus, religious difference is not necessarily irreconcilable nor an obstacle for following the way of love.

— 26 —

Did Jesus Exclude the Samaritans?

IN this rather long chapter, we will be discussing Jesus' interaction with a Samaritan woman at Jacob's Well. It is well-known story from the Gospel of John.

Instead of including the long passage from John 4, I invite you all to get out your Bibles like you would in an old-school Baptist church and turn to John 4 and read verses 3–42. And after you do so, return to this page and let us delve deep into this story of Jesus' intriguing conversation with the Samaritan woman.

Well-Water Talk

As the story goes, Jesus is traveling from Judea in the South to his home in Galilee in the North. In between Judea and Galilee is Samaria. Weary from his sojourn, he stops midway in the city of Sychar in Samaria. Sychar is significant because on the outskirts of the city is Jacob's Well, which Jacob himself dug. Jesus sits aside the well and rests. His disciples go into town for lunch.

Jesus is alone and a Samaritan woman comes to draw water. This is not surprising. It is a town in Samaria after all. What *is* surprising is that Jesus talks to her. Samaritans and Galileans don't usually do this.

Jesus asks her for a drink of water from Jacob's Well. He doesn't command it. That it is *Jacob's* well is important. Samaritans, Judeans, and Galileans (which Jesus is) all share Jacob as a patriarch of their ethnic religions.

The Samaritan woman is surprised by Jesus' request for water. She can tell Jesus is not a Samaritan somehow, most likely because of his dialect. She believes he is *Ioudaios*, a Greek label usually translated "Jew." Virtually all biblical translations translate this as "Jew." But there is a great deal of nuance to the label *Ioudaios*. It's meaning depends a great deal on context and focus. David Bentley Hart translates *Ioudaios* as "Judeans." (We will discuss this in depth below.)

The Samaritan woman says, "You are an *Ioudaios*; I am a Samaritan [from Samaria]. We're not supposed to be talking." Interestingly, Jesus ignores this point of division. He also doesn't clarify that he is a Galilean and not specifically from Judea. He wants to talk about more pressing matters, matters of the heart. He replies, "If you recognized God's gift and who it is saying to you 'Give me a drink,' you would have asked him and he would have given you living water."

The Samaritan woman retorts, "Lord, you have no bucket and the well is deep; so where do you get the living water from? Surely you are not greater than our Father Jacob, who gave us the well, and drank from it himself, and his sons and livestock too?"

The New Jacob

This is a profoundly meaningful statement. The Samaritan woman, following Jesus' lead, avoids what divides them. She seems to leave their divisions aside, which she initially was focusing on, and goes to unity. She in fact claims camaraderie between herself and Jesus. "We share Jacob," she proclaims. "*Our* Father Jacob, who gave *us* this well."

She then asks an important question. "Are you greater than Father Jacob," the one who unites us? Are you going to supersede our Jacob connection and resort to what divides us?

Jesus implies an answer of "yes." He is going to replace that old connection with a new connection. Basically, Jesus claims that whereas Jacob's Well gives regular water that will leave a person thirsty eventually, *my* well gives a water "that gives the life of ages."

The Samaritan woman indeed wants this water. Who wouldn't? Who enjoys being really thirsty and having to get and lug water around?

It is crucial to see what Jesus is doing here. Jesus is basically staking claim as a New Jacob whose well gives *living* water. Not only that, he is claiming that his position of New Jacob will, like the original Jacob, unite

Samaritans and Judeans in their real common source, Yahweh. The woman and Jesus share a religious father, Jacob. In Jacob there is unity. Jesus as the New Jacob returns them to the space before the divide, to unity, to Yahweh.

Jesus then breaks the religious language and talk of Jacob by saying, "Go and get your husband and come back." We find out in the following back-and-forth that the woman doesn't have a husband, that she's been married five times (we don't know why, whether divorce or death), and that her cohabitant is not her sixth. Jesus doesn't judge her. This New Jacob is a person of grace and forgiveness.

The Samaritan woman is impressed by Jesus' insight and intuition about her and her life. She asserts, "Lord, I see that you are a prophet." Then, she changes the subject, it seems. In fact, she changes tactics again. She reverts to division, maybe piqued at his calling out her five marriages and unmarried status. She says, "Our fathers worshipped on this mountain; and you people say that the place where it is necessary to worship is in Jerusalem."

Jesus responds with a mini-sermon. It is the heart of the text. All before leads up to this text. Everything after this text is influenced by it. That it comes in the middle of the story suggests this.

Worship Differentiated

> "Trust me, madam, an hour is coming when you will worship the Father neither on this mountain nor in Jerusalem. You people worship [what or who] you do not know, we worship [what or who] we know; because salvation is from the Judaeans; But an hour comes, and now is, when the true worshippers will worship the Father in spirit and truth; for indeed the Father looks for those worshipping him so; God is spirit, and it is necessary that those worshipping worship in spirit and truth." (John 4:21–24)

Because these words of Jesus are so central, we need to discuss it in detail.

First, what is striking in this passage of a few sentences is the number of times the word "worship" (*proskyneō*) appears. It appears eight times. This fact alone tells us that *worship* is the focus of Jesus' mini-sermon.

Jesus begins his mini-sermon with a crucial line. "An hour is coming when you will worship the Father neither on this mountain nor in Jerusalem."

Did Jesus Exclude the Samaritans?

Remember, a central difference between Samaritan and Judean-Galilean faith is that the former sees Mount Gerizim as the center of the universe and the latter sees Jerusalem as the center. Jesus is transcending this divide with his statement. Gerzim, Jerusalem—neither of our people are correct, Jesus seems to say. Our *worship of God*, period, will one day unite us.

Jesus then differentiates their people's worship. "You—Samaritans—worship [*hos*] you do not know. We worship [*hos*] we know." Hart and all other translators translate *hos* as "what" so that we get, "You worship what you do not know. We worship what we know." But *hos* can also be translated "who" so that we get, "You worship *who* you do not know. We worship *who* we know." *Hos* as "who" makes more sense.

This statement—"You as a Samaritan worship who you do not know and we Judean Galileans worship who we do know"—is a theological statement of fact. I don't see Jesus' words as a criticism of Samaritan faith necessarily. Samaritans would agree that they worship a God they cannot fully know. Samaritans, as we discussed, see God as *unknowable*, ineffable, wholly transcendent. For Samaritans, Yahweh is unknowable, one whom even the faithful do not fully know. However, they still *worship* Yahweh. They may see God as unknowable, but they still *worship* him. And worship, the act of humbling oneself before God, itself is an honorable and obedient thing to do.

For Jesus, that he, his disciples, and his people worship a God that is knowable is also true. This is especially true for those who know God as Father and preach God as Father, like Jesus does. In his case, the God worshipped is one who is especially close and knowable, as close as a father is to his family.

Samaritans worship a Yahweh that is unknowable. Judeans and Galileans worship a Yahweh that is knowable, as knowable as a father is knowable. These are statements of theological fact.

Then Jesus says something that at first blush seems to surely be an exclusivist claim: "Because salvation is from the [*Ioudaios*]." However, this passage is not as simple or straightforward as it would seem.

Judean or Jew?

Ioudaios is a very difficult word to translate. It can refer to someone from the place known as Judea, a province that has Jerusalem at its center. *Ioudaios* can also refer to someone practicing the ethnic religion that includes following Torah, worshipping Yahweh, and considering yourself part of Israel. In this second meaning, *Ioudaios* share Israel and Jacob, Israel's namesake.

Things are further complicated by the fact that some Samaritans considered themselves *Ioudaios*.[1] And there was a time surrounding Jesus' time in which, politically speaking, *Ioudaios* incorporated Galilee and Samaria. Judaism scholar Morton Smith gives us a list of what *Ioudaios* could have referred to:

> For clarity, we may recall that the three main earlier meanings were:
>
> (1) one of the descendants of the patriarch Judah, i.e. (if in the male line) a member of the tribe of Judah;
>
> (2) a native of Judaea, a "Judaean";
>
> (3) a "Jew", i.e. a member of Yahweh's chosen people, entitled to participate in those religious ceremonies to which only such members were admitted.
>
> Now appears the new, fourth meaning:
>
> (4) a member of the Judaeo-Samaritan-Idumaean-Ituraean-Galilean alliance.[2]

Yet another complicating factor is the fact that if *Ioudaios* refers to someone living in Judea, then Jesus himself would not qualify. Jesus was a Galilean through and through.

So, what does Jesus mean when he says "salvation comes from *Ioudaios*"? Does he refer to the place or to the religion of Jacob?

I think Jesus is referring to the latter. But not in the modern sense. He is referring to the ancient *Ioudaios* who practiced the way of God. He is referring to those who forged the faith of Jacob/Israel and its way of salvation. Jesus referring to the religious meaning of *Ioudaios* allows him to include himself as a Galilean (and not a Judean) with the term.

I also believe Jesus includes Samaritans in the term *Ioudaios*. He includes Samaritans not merely in a political alliance, but a religio-political one called "the kingdom of God."

Jesus seems to say to the Samaritan woman, "You refer to *Ioudaios* and compare them to Samaritans [*Samaratis* in Greek] and point to what divides us. But I am referring to something more ancient and lasting and uniting. I am referring to the origin of our salvation, those ancient, faithful

---

1. Joshua Garoway, *Paul's Gentile-Jews*, 43
2. Morton Smith, *Cambridge History of Judaism, Volume 3*, 210

followers of God's way in whose lineage we stand, a lineage I am here to embody."

Let Us Meet at Jacob's Well

Could it be that Jesus is saying something like this in John 4:22?: "You all as Samaritans *worship* God but as unknowable; we *worship* God but as knowable; we both *worship God* because salvation originated from the descendants of Jacob." The focus then becomes the fact that both worship God and both derive from Jacob, whose well they are right next to.

Again, the location of the conversation—Jacob's Well—is key. It is here where Jacob pitched a tent, created an altar in order to worship God, and called that altar El-Elohe-Israel—Almighty God of Israel. This is another point of mutuality.

Samaritans and Judeans both go back to the same center where true worship of God is born: Israel. Of note, Israel is a name later given to Jacob. Samaritans and Judeans share a common father, Jacob/Israel.

As I mentioned, one reason to doubt that Jesus means *Ioudaios* in the specific sense of being from Judea is that Jesus is a Galilean. Jesus, as a Galilean, would have likely viewed Judea just as suspiciously as a Samaritan would have. We see this suspicion in how Jesus interacts with the Pharisees, who were centered in Judea and represented Judean Judaism. In other words, Galileans and Samaritans both experienced political and cultural tension with Judea. Hence, a reference to salvation coming from Judea as in Judeans or "modern Judean Judaism" seems unlikely to me. Jesus is actively resisting "Judean Judaism" by talking with the Samaritan woman. It simply makes more sense that Jesus is using the generic meaning of *Ioudaios* as pointing to faithful followers of the primordial faith of Israel/Jacob.

All of this is to say, Jesus is pointing to worship and the shared tie to the shared salvation offered by God. He is pointing to a uniting God worshipped by Jacob and Jacob's sons and by both Samaritans and Judean-Galileans. And he is proclaiming himself to be the New Jacob. Like the old Jacob, he wants to unite and root Samaria, Judea, and his own Galilee again in the single source of God, the God of Israel.

The opening sentence of his mini-sermon thus makes clearer sense. On the ground of God is where salvation resides, not in Jerusalem or at Mount Gerizim.

God as Father and Spirit

It doesn't stop there. Jesus goes on to further harmonize the two houses divided from one another. Jesus says, "The true worshippers will worship the Father in spirit and truth; for indeed the Father looks for those worshipping him so; God is spirit, and it is necessary that those worshipping worship in spirit and truth."

"Father" is how Jesus sees God. On the other hand, the Samaritan school sees God as pure spirit and balk at human-based titles and notions for God, such as human fatherliness. At the end of his mini-sermon, Jesus connects and harmonizes the two, Father and Spirit. God is Father but God is also Spirit. Truth is found in them both. Jesus seems to be saying, "Let us unite in the true worship of Father God, who is also Spirit."

The amazing discussion around Jacob's Well ends with the woman saying, "I know that the Messiah is coming—the one called Anointed—when that one arrives he will announce all things to us."

Jesus quips, "I am he: I who am speaking to you." Jesus seems to say, "I just explained it all to you. You don't need to search any longer." Before she answers, the disciples arrive.

The Good Samaritan II

The conversation switches to one between Jesus and his disciples after they return from lunch. They arrive and see Jesus talking with the Samaritan woman. They interestingly ignore this odd scene. It is not anything unusual. This is what Jesus does: talks to strangers and seeks transformation in them.

Again not judged, this time by the disciples, the Samaritan woman leaves to go into town. She forgets her water jug but doesn't come back for it. She trusts the situation enough not to worry about it. The jug is also something she no longer needs, her thirst quenched by the living water of Jesus' well. So she goes into town to tell everyone about Jesus, wondering if this is the Messiah they've been waiting for.

Meanwhile, the disciples nag Jesus to eat. But Jesus talks about another hunger. He says, "I have food to eat of which you do not know."

This statement to his disciples seems to parallel his earlier statement to the Samaritan woman. "I have food to eat of which you do not know" sounds a lot like "I have water that you don't know anything about." These

Did Jesus Exclude the Samaritans?

similar refrains seem to connect and compare the disciples and the Samaritan woman. Jesus goes on to compare them in another kind of mini-sermon.

> "My food is that I may do the will of the one who has sent me and may bring his work to completion. Do you not say, 'Four months yet, and then comes the harvest'? I tell you, Look, lift up your eyes and see the fields, because they are already white for harvesting. The reaper is receiving wages and gathering fruit for life in the Age, so that the one sowing and the one reaping may rejoice together. For in this the saying is true: 'That one is the sower and another the reaper.' I have sent you to reap that for which you have not labored, and you have entered into their labor."

A field to harvest is the food equivalent of a well to get water from. The field is ripe and ready to harvest. The seeds were planted by the prophets, the sages, and the patriarchs, by the anointed ones before and the Anointed One now, from Jacob to the New Jacob. The field to harvest is the kingdom and the life of ages it brings.

Jesus points to those who are already on the case, those already doing the work of harvesting the fully ripened field. The implication is the Samaritan woman is harvesting the field.

We have another case where a "good Samaritan" is lifted up as exemplifying the way of God. She is in town telling her friends that she has found the Anointed One. She is harvesting the field and reaping the reward of the life of ages. "What are you doing, dear disciples?" That is what Jesus seems to infer.

We see Jesus' meaning clarified by the harvest the Samaritan woman brings in. "Many of the Samaritans of that city had faith in him on account of the woman testifying."

Jesus stays two more days ministering to the Samaritan people. The story ends with these wonderful words of universal restorationist fervor: "We know that this man is truly the savior of the cosmos."

We've gone from the restoration of unity between two peoples deemed enemies to the future restoration of unity between all people. This restoration of unity comes via a Savior who envisions all people joining together.

— 27 —

Who Is Excluded from the Commonwealth?

JESUS, particularly compared to the religious of his day, envisioned and cultivated an expansive community. Religious, cultural, and ethnic differences mattered less than a humble and compassionate heart. In fact, these two heart conditions, humility and compassion, were the key to entering the kingdom.

In the Gospels, Jesus again and again welcomes and includes those who've exhibited commitment to the way of self-emptying compassion. Sinners and those regarded as spiritually impure and incorrect? Included. Gentiles living in a Gentile region? Included. Polytheistic members of the Roman government? Included. Jewish in background yet spiritually exiled for working with the Roman government? Included. Healers ministering to people in the name of Jesus though not his direct disciples? Included. Samaritans seen as pariah by the religious establishment? Included. All included.

That said, Jesus does have standards or requirements for who is included. We are not talking cheap grace here. Jesus did in fact exclude those who did not meet the standard or requirement. But religious background, culture, and faith claims were not primary factors in Jesus' decision to include or exclude.

The basis for who is included or excluded relates not to one's religion or one's identity per se. The basis relates to what one *does*. The basis of orthopraxis—correct practice—is seen most clearly in maybe Jesus' most provocative parable.

Sheep Safe, Goats Out

The following passage is lengthy. Nonetheless, I am quoting it whole piece. It is such a key teaching as well as one of the most eminent. It of course comes from Matthew 25.

> "And when the Son of Man comes in his glory, and all the angels with him, then he will sit on his throne of glory; And all the nations will be assembled before him, and he will separate them from one another, as the shepherd separates the sheep from the kid goats, and will set the sheep to his right, but the kid goats to the left. Then the King will say to those to his right, 'Come, you blessed by my Father, inherit the Kingdom prepared for you from the foundation of the cosmos. For I was hungry and you gave me something to eat, I was thirsty and you gave me drink, I was a stranger and you gave me hospitality, Naked and you clothed me, I was ill and you looked after me, I was in prison and you came to me.' Then the just will answer him, saying, 'When did we see you hungry and feed you, or thirsty and give you drink? And when did we see you a stranger and give you hospitality, or naked and clothe you? And when did we see you ill or in prison and come to you?' And in reply the King will say to them, 'Amen, I tell you, inasmuch as you did it to one of the least of these my brothers, you did it to me.' Then he will say to those to the left, 'Go from me, you execrable ones, into the fire of the Age prepared for the Slanderer and his angels. For I was hungry and you did not give me anything to eat, I was thirsty and you did not give me drink, I was a stranger and you did not give me hospitality, naked and you did not clothe me, ill and in prison and you did not look after me.' Then they too will answer, saying, 'Lord, when did we see you hungry or thirsty or a stranger or naked or ill or in prison, and did not attend to you?' Then he will answer them, saying, 'Amen, I tell you, inasmuch as you did not do it to one of the least of these my brothers, neither did you do it to me.' And these will go to the chastening of that Age, but the just to the life of that Age."

Jesus symbolizes the nations that are included as the sheep and the nations that are excluded as the goats. In the coming age, the heavenly king will separate each into one or the other category. On what basis? We discuss this question below (after a word about biblical translation).

Translation Matters

I've used David Bentley Hart's translation above of Matthew 25. Hart's goal in his new translation of the New Testament was to offer a literal translation that is not influenced by preconceived notions of modern, evangelical orthodoxy. Thus, instead of loosely translating the Greek word *aiōnios* as "eternal," he translates it literally. *Aiōnios* is a word from which we get the English word "eon." It means "eons long" or "ages long." The Greek word for "eternal" as we understand it is *aidios*, a word that does not appear in Matthew 25 and that Jesus rarely ever uses unless referring to God or something in relationship to God, who alone is eternal.

Wherein most Bible translations we see the phrases "eternal life" or "eternal punishment," in Hart's more direct translation we see "life of ages" and "chastening of ages." Hart's translation may seem awkward because we've gotten used to so many misleading translations, beginning in many ways with the King James Version in 1611. But Hart offers us a literal translation that gets at the most specific meaning of the word *aiōnios*.

Jesus' Benchmark

Matthew 25 seems rather straightforward. What decides the fate of a nation or, by inference, an individual is how they respond to the pain and suffering of the most vulnerable. The sheep respond out of humility and with compassion and are included. The goats do not and are excluded.

If one treats the most vulnerable with humility and compassion, Jesus declares, "come and inherit the kingdom prepared for you." Why are the most vulnerable the benchmark? Because the image of God, God's self, principally resides in the most vulnerable. The fact that divinity resides so powerfully in the thoroughly vulnerable Galilean named Jesus shows us that God resides most poignantly in the most vulnerable. Therefore, what is done for and unto the most vulnerable is done for and unto God.

If one ignores the most vulnerable and does not choose the way of self-emptying compassion, failing to help where help is needed, King Jesus commands, "go into the execrable fire of the age." Ignoring the most vulnerable amounts to ignoring God, for God's image resides in the most vulnerable.

Approaching others, especially the most vulnerable, with an intentional vulnerability of our own, and applying this core state of being when and where it is needed—that is Jesus' benchmark. Jesus calls us to a life of vulnerability defined by humility and compassion.

"What about faith?" good Lutherans ask. "You seem to be offering up 'works salvation' instead of salvation by faith."

Faith is presumed in the state of being humble and compassionate. Faith is an insight into the truth of God's love and an internalization of that love. Faith is letting love in. And if love is let in, love naturally flows out. Letting love in, we in turn humble ourselves and get our selfish ways out of the way. Self-emptied, love breathes through us.

This is the faith described in the paradigm Jesus gives us in Matthew 25. Faith here amounts to internalizing the fundamental truth that God is Love and that God calls us to respond with love. If humility and compassion don't naturally flow from our faith, our faith is only partial and not full.

The Concise Case for Universalism

Seeing suffering and responding with compassion is the benchmark for Jesus. What if we apply this benchmark of inclusion, this benchmark of self-emptying compassion, to God? If God sees such acute suffering like the nation in the parable, if God sees the hellish existence of those experiencing eons of divine chastening, and turns away and ignores this suffering from God's throne in heaven, how does God meet Jesus' benchmark? And if God doesn't meet the benchmark, then Jesus is wrong.

Thankfully, the teaching of universal restoration submits that God responds using the benchmark Jesus gives in Matthew 25. God will seek to end the suffering. And what God seeks, God finds. What God wants, God gets. To borrow from the psalmist, hell may last for a nighttime, but heaven comes in the morning.

— 28 —

Unforgivable-Sin Exclusion

THERE is another distinct, undeniable example of Jesus excluding. This example of exclusivity seems irreversible. The example comes in the Gospel of Matthew as well, 12:31–32:

> "Hence I tell you, every sin and blasphemy will be excused men, but the blasphemy of the Spirit will not be excused. And whoever speaks a word against the Son of Man, it will be excused him; but whoever speaks against the Spirit, the Holy One, it will not be excused him, neither in this age nor in the one that is coming."

Again, the punishment is not eternal. The word translated "age" here is *aiōn*, the singular form of *aiōnios*, "ages." The age to come has a duration. The duration is uncertain, but there is a beginning and an end. Nonetheless, there *is* hell to pay.

Basically, for Jesus, the action of speaking against the Holy Spirit will not be tolerated nor excused. Every other sin and blasphemy, including against Jesus, will be excused and forgiven. But if it's against the Holy Spirit, all deals are off. Why, I wonder?

Holy Spirit, the Transforming One

The reason speaking against the Holy Spirit is so bad relates to the role the Holy Spirit plays. The Holy Spirit is responsible for moving us to a transformed life of humbly and compassionately approaching the world. The Holy Spirit moves in the hearts of men and women and leads these hearts to a life in God. And, to quote Bono of U2, "She moves in mysterious ways," namely diverse and myriad ways.

To diss the Holy Spirit, who is responsible for this holy work, means to dismiss the work the Holy Spirit does, to dismiss the change the Holy Spirit works in people's hearts. Such dismissal exhibits a disregard for the transformation of others. It also limits the movement of God in the world.

Church-Bearer and Pluralism's Source

The Holy Spirit has other central tasks. Jesus declared that the Holy Spirit, the Spirit of Truth, will pervade the world when he leaves that world and guide and comfort his disciples. The church was born because of the pervasive breath of the Holy Spirit of Truth. The Holy Spirit breathed and kept breathing life into the church just as she breathed life into creation and us, God's image-carriers.

The Holy Spirit is also the godhead whose movement transcends religious specificity and boundaries. The Spirit of Truth is the source of the wisdom and compassion found in non-Christian religions.

Seeing all the Holy Spirit is and does, Jesus submits that to call the Holy Spirit a lie is to call into question these crucial functions. To call the Holy Spirit a lie is to call the presence of the Spirit of Truth a fiction, the church's life imaginary, and the Spirit's boundarylessness and boundlessness a lie.

Breath-Infuser

More than this, Jesus sees the Holy Spirit as the protector against nihilism. We see this when we consider an alternative translation of the Greek word *pneuma*, usually translated "spirit."

Pneuma can be translated as "breath" as well. Using the translation of breath helps us to understand Jesus' reasoning for completely condemning blasphemy regarding the Holy Spirit.

To blaspheme the Holy Breath, which gives us breath and gives us life, is to denigrate the preciousness and sacredness of life itself and not just the Creator of life. Denigrating the source of life means denigrating the gift of life as well. That is sacrilegious at its gravest level. It amounts to a form of nihilism, for it denigrates and denies the source of breath and the gift of breath in us the living.

— 29 —

The Child Test

A SIGNIFICANT and recurrent example Jesus offers to show who's in and who's out is children. Jesus on a few occasions lifts up children as the model for inclusion in God's commonwealth. Jesus also expresses great disdain and harsh judgment for those who harm the psyche of a child. Matthew 18 says this:

> At that hour, the disciples approached Jesus, saying, "Who then is the greater in the Kingdom of the heavens?" And, calling a child forward, he stood the child in their midst, and said, "Amen, I tell you, unless you turn back and become as children, you most certainly may not enter into the Kingdom of the heavens. He therefore who will make himself small as this child, this one is the greater in the Kingdom of the heavens. And whoever welcomes one such child in my name welcomes me; And, whoever causes one of these little ones who have faith in me to falter, it is better for him to have a millstone, of the kind turned by an ass, hung about his neck, and to be drowned in the depths of the sea."

It is hard to miss how severe Jesus sees the harming and hindering of a child. Jesus says the penalty will be worse than a purposeful and extended drowning! Is this endless? No. Is there restorative justice on the other end? Yes, all things will be restored to God. But the penalty is severe and lengthy.

More significantly, Jesus points to children as the exemplification of the humble and compassionate life.

The Humble Society

We don't often hear it said, but a just and compassionate society must be, first and foremost, humble. The commonwealth of God, a just and compassionate society, begins with humility, with seeing our singular selves as part of a common self, a community of selves. The word "common-wealth" says it all. Individual autonomy and self-sufficiency are important, but the goal is common wealth, shared wealth, shared prosperity. To get to that goal requires humility, a practice of putting others and the Holy Other first.

Jesus points to the commonwealth of God as first and foremost humble. He does this by claiming children to be the model not only of faith but also of citizenship in the commonwealth of God. If you want to know what it means to be a citizen in God's commonwealth, look at children. The Gospel of Luke shows us this.

> People were also bringing babies to Jesus for him to place his hands on them. When the disciples saw this, they rebuked them. But Jesus called the children to him and said, "Let the little children come to me, and do not hinder them, for the kingdom of God belongs to such as these. Truly I tell you, anyone who will not receive the kingdom of God like a little child will never enter it." (Luke 18:15–17, NIV)

Then in Luke 22, during the Last Supper, this is what Jesus has to say:

> A dispute also arose among them as to which of them was considered to be greatest. Jesus said to them, "The kings of the Gentiles lord it over them; and those who exercise authority over them call themselves Benefactors. But you are not to be like that. Instead, the greatest among you should be like the youngest, and the one who rules like the one who serves. For who is greater, the one who is at the table or the one who serves? Is it not the one who is at the table? But I am among you as one who serves." (Luke 22:24–27, NIV)

Children are the perfect exemplars of humility, Jesus tells us. The children are not just our perfect model, they are, they must be, the ultimate measure of how just and compassionate we are.

Ending Where We Began

The way of the child that Jesus preached and lived means internalizing the commonwealth of God with wonder and beauty, exuberance and vulnerability, and living our faith with honesty void of self-consciousness and overthinking. This is the way Jesus lived.

Childlikeness, receptivity, humility, and vulnerability—these things never left Jesus. The newborn in the manger continued into adulthood.

As Jesus contemplated his heavenly Father's work in the world and in his heart, he was continuously born anew. I imagine the carpenter Jesus working with wood. To use William Blake's words, I imagine Jesus seeing a world in each grain of wood he sanded. I imagine he experienced eternity in each of those sweat-soaked hours. I imagine he saw heaven in the wild flowers he passed on his way home. I imagine him smiling as he held a neighbor's baby in his arms, knowing he held Infinity. He pondered these things in his heart, like his mother did when he was in her womb. Jesus lived and perfected the perfection of a newborn, the humility of a child, the accepting nature of a little one. In turn, he teaches us, urges us, to do the same.

Compassion is a natural outgrowth of humility. Humility enables us to sense when compassion is needed. Humility means our self and selfishness is put aside and out of the way. The empty space allows us to better look and see the many human needs in front of us and respond with compassion.

Jesus embodies this truth again and again in the Gospels. His whole life was about putting aside self and in turn seeing the human condition, the pain of another, and the need for compassion.

Eleven times in the Gospels Jesus is said to have looked deeply at people or crowds of people and felt "moved by inward compassion." These eleven times initiated a miracle event. While we modernists may question the actuality of natural laws being counteracted, we should not fail to see the heart of these miracle stores. Jesus' insight and his corresponding compassion gave way to him tending to another's hurt and helping in another's healing.

Children again model this as well. Children are naturally empathetic. They are better at seeing pain and hurt in another. What's more, they possess less of a filter when it comes to asking for help.

Epilogue

A Beautiful Day's Bells

September 11, 2001, New York City

I WAS new to New York City in September 2001. My wife happened to be in Florida with family and would fly to New York just a week later on September 18.

The sky was, as Bruce Springsteen sings, an "unbelievable blue" that Tuesday morning. It was an unbelievably beautiful day in New York.

Then the world changed.

My first class at Union Theological Seminary was scheduled for that Tuesday morning, at 9 a.m. Class was cancelled.

Union Seminary is fortunately some four miles uptown from where the Twin Towers were. However, Manhattan is a small island of interconnections. Uptown we heard the sirens, saw the smoke, saw the dazed and panicked faces arise from the subway and walk along Broadway. Columbia's Presbyterian hospital soon filled with people looking to give blood or to help in some way.

I, new to the city and uncertain of what was happening, was beyond scared. Once it became clear that it was a terrorist attack, my mind went to the Jewish Theological Seminary, open and unprotected just across the street from Union. It was an easy target and too close, and politically significant for a terrorist. Then there was Riverside Church, whose steeple is nothing compared to the Twin Towers but on the Upper Westside it reaches high and symbolically.

The sounds of military planes that soon filled the sky also became worrisome. How do you tell the difference between a military plane flying overhead and a terrorist-hijacked plane flying as a bullet toward you?

Missing-person flyers soon started going up. Photos of persons with the word "missing" above or below them, pinned to trees, poles, bus stops, they served as ubiquitous symbols of tragedy and hope, a hope beyond hope, a heartbroken hope, a hope eventually deferred.

One flyer I saw is burned in my memory. One of the most beautiful faces I ever saw. A face Michelangelo could not turn away from . . . "Missing."

I also remember watching *The Today Show* a few days later. A young wife was talking about her husband lost in the Twin Towers attack. They had just celebrated their seventh anniversary the day before, September 10, 1994. The day my wife and I were married. September 10, 2001, a happy seventh celebrated.

September 11, 2001. 9/11. Their marriage broken in two without reason. Ours still standing by the grace of God, or a less gracious fate, I don't know.

Broken Bell Interlude

Through the fall and winter, the carillon bells of Riverside Church continued to stand silent. Broken bells cannot sing. And this was fine with me.

For months after 9/11, I could not listen to music. Music, which had always been a source of healing and joy, always an indelible part of my life—I could not bear to hear it. Music seemed too easy, too entertaining, too ideal. There seemed to be no note or musical phrase that made any sense nor helped me make any sense of the tragedy. To listen to music would hence be an escape, an escape I could not conscientiously condone. I was one of the fortunate ones and did not deserve such a naïve anesthetic away from reality. That's the kind of effect 9/11 had on even the "lucky ones."

It was a long, long winter.

Then spring arrived. Then Easter arrived.

Epilogue
Easter, March 31, 2002, New York City

3/31 for me began with quiet. I was not up to the show of Easter at church. I had been skipping church for weeks. Going to an Easter service seemed too easy a penance.

The morning itself would become my Easter service. The morning ritual of making coffee was the prelude. The gurgling and dripping of the coffee maker served as preparation for sounds to come. The coffee and I ready, I prepared the day's first cup of coffee as if the invocation. Each sip became a little prayer. Each moment in between, a meditation.

Then the reborn bells of Riverside Church sounded. They filled the morning air with an ecstatic flourish. There was no rhyme or reason to the music, just sound sounding and pervading. It scared me at first. But then I simply listened and smiled. The heavenly sound echoed all along Claremont and Broadway and through the whole of Morningside Heights and across the Hudson. It pierced my heart. And as the vibrations of sound gave way to vibrations of sound, I cried like a child, completely vulnerable yet completely embraced.

On that same sunny, crisp, church-less Sunday morning, I opened the CD player's dusty door. Inside, secure and replete with possibilities, U2's *All That You Can't Leave Behind* rested. It too survived through the winter. It too was opened to a new day. I hit play. The first track, "Beautiful Day," peeled.

> The heart is a bloom
> Shoots up through the stony ground . . .
> And see the bird with a leaf in her mouth
> After the flood all the colors came out . . .
> It's a beautiful day

Bibliography

Boyarin, Daniel. *The Jewish Gospels: The Story of the Jewish Christ*. New York: New Press, 2013.
Chilton, Bruce. *Rabbi Jesus: An Intimate Biography*. New York: Doubleday, 2000.
Cobb, John B. *Jesus' Abba: The God Who Has Not Failed*. Minneapolis: Fortress, 2016.
Cone, James H. *The Spirituals and the Blues: An Interpretation*. New York: Orbis, 1992.
Dunn, James D. G. *Christology in the Making: A New Testament Inquiry into the Origins of the Doctrine of the Incarnation*. Grand Rapids: Eerdmans, 1996.
Ehrman, Bart D. "Did Nazareth Exist?" *The Bart Ehrman Blog*, March 1, 2015. https://ehrmanblog.org/did-nazareth-exist.
———. *How Jesus Became God: The Exaltation of a Preacher from Galilee*. New York: HarperOne, 2014.
———. "How Jesus Became God, part 1,." Lecture, posted March 30, 2016. https://youtube.com/7IPAKsGbqcg.
Francis, Pope. "Pope at Mass: Culture of Encounter Is the Foundation of Peace." Vatican Radio, May 22, 2013. https://web.archive.org/web/20130522145031/http://en.radiovaticana.va/news/2013/05/22/pope_at_mass:_culture_of_encounter_is_the_foundation_of_peace/en1-694445.
Garoway, Joshua. *Paul's Gentile-Jews: Neither Jew nor Gentile, but Both*. London: Palgrave Macmillan, 2012.
Hart, David Bentley. *The New Testament: A Translation*. New Haven, CT: Yale University Press, 2017.
Hattrup, Kathleen N. "Crying Little Boy Asks Pope If His Atheist Dad Could Be in Heaven." *Aleteia*, April 16, 2018. https://aleteia.org/2018/04/16/crying-little-boy-asks-pope-if-his-atheist-dad-could-be-in-heaven/.
King, Martin Luther, Jr. "Letter from a Birmingham Jail." In *A Testament of Hope: The Essential Writings of Martin Luther King, Jr.*, edited by James Melvin Washington, 289–302. San Francisco: HarperSanFrancisco, 1991.
Marcin, Tim. "Pope Francis Hugs, Comforts Little Boy Who Asked If His Atheist Dad Was in Heaven." *Newsweek*, April 18, 2018. https://www.newsweek.com/pope-francis-hugs-comforts-little-boy-who-asked-atheist-dad-was-heaven-891113.
Martin, Colin. "The Gods of the Imperial Roman." *History Today* 19 (April 4, 1969) 255–63.

Bibliography

McKenzie, Alycia. "Commentary on Mark 7:24–37." http://www.workingpreacher.org/preaching.aspx?commentary_id=391.

Pasulka, Diana W. "Virtual Religion: Popular Culture and the Digital World." In *Religion: Sources, Perspectives, and Methodologies*, edited by Jeffrey J. Kripal, 325–40. London: Macmillan, 2015.

Pinnock, Clark. *The Grace of God, the Will of Man*. Grand Rapids: Zondervan, 1989.

Smail, Tom. *Once and For All: A Confession of the Cross*. Eugene, OR: Wipf & Stock, 2005.

Smith, Morton. "The Gentiles in Judaism 125 BCE – 66 CE." In *Cambridge History of Judaism*, edited by William Horbury et al., vol. 3, 192–249. Cambridge: Cambridge University Press, 2000.

White, L. Michael. "The Roman Empire and Judea." *From Jesus to Christ*, Frontline, April 1998. https://www.pbs.org/wgbh/pages/frontline/shows/religion/portrait/jews.html.

Wojnicki, Ann. "More than Just a Parable: The Genetic History of the Samaritans." *23andMeBlog*, September 5, 2008. https://blog.23andme.com/23andme-and-you/genetics-101/more-than-just-a-parable-the-genetic-history-of-the-samaritans/.

www.ingramcontent.com/pod-product-compliance
Lightning Source LLC
Chambersburg PA
CBHW070917180426

43192CB00037B/1652